# AMERICAN
# FARMERS' MOVEMENTS

---

## FRED A. SHANNON

*Professor of History*
*University of Illinois*

---

## AN ANVIL ORIGINAL

*under the general editorship of*

## LOUIS L. SNYDER

---

HD
1761
.S48

## VAN NOSTRAND COMPANY, INC.

### PRINCETON, NEW JERSEY

RONTO                                                    LONDON

### NEW YORK

In memory of
Edna

D. VAN NOSTRAND COMPANY, INC.

120 Alexander St., Princeton, New Jersey (*Principal office*)
257 Fourth Avenue, New York 10, New York
25 Hollinger Rd., Toronto 16, Canada
358, Kensington High Street, London, W.14, England

COPYRIGHT, ©, 1957, BY
FRED A. SHANNON

Library of Congress Catalog Card No. 57-12488

PRINTED IN THE UNITED STATES OF AMERICA

# PREFACE

THERE has been no full-length account of farmers' movements in America from the beginning to the present, written from a strictly historical point of view, and this discussion will not fill the gap. It is of necessity too brief. Even monographic literature for the colonial period is spotty, and one often has to rely on the larger general histories of the colonies, individually and as a group, or on the source materials. Secondary literature is most complete for the years after 1865.

In reproducing the documents, I followed the printed sources as faithfully as I knew how, except for perhaps half a dozen obviously typographical errors that pedantry alone would excuse repeating, such as "fo" for "of," or a singular subject with a plural verb in the writing of an obviously literate man. On two or three occasions I indicated elisions rather than repeat an illiterate usage that added nothing to the sense.

Drs. Robert H. Jones and Helen K. Reinhart were of immense help to me in the uncovering and submission of innumerable documents for me to cull out, and in detecting my errors in reproduction. Blame me alone for any mistakes that remain. Miss Virginia R. Grollemond also supplied some documents.

*Urbana, Illinois*
*August, 1957*

FRED A. SHANNON

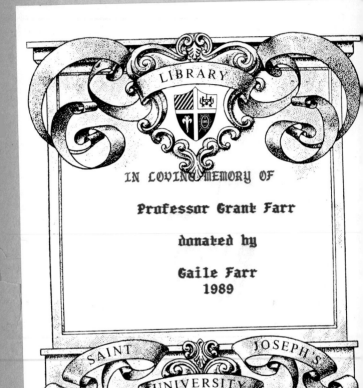

# TABLE OF CONTENTS

# Part One

# AMERICAN FARMERS' MOVEMENTS

# — 1 —

# INTRODUCTION

**The Ups and Downs of Farmers.** Regardless of how much wealth the speculators, landlords, moneylenders, merchants, and transportation agencies may have wrested from the products of the soil, the actual tiller, unless involved in some of these other activities, has only occasionally done better than make a bare living. Farming was a way of life and not a road to opulence. During great wars such as the Revolution, the Civil War, and the huge conflicts of the twentieth century, the increased demand on the farmer led to rising prices that were generally illusory. In each of these cases the monetary and price inflation led to expansion on a credit basis, the debts to be paid later when money was scarce and prices were low. In the most recent instance, unsettled world conditions and a state of constant preparedness for war since 1945 have held in check much but not all of the reaction.

There has been much talk about farmers living from hand to mouth all their lives, yet making a big profit from the constant increase in value of their land. This contention is largely nonsense. In the first place, for nearly three centuries in America a good share of them all were constantly on the move. Many were squatters on the public domain who ultimately had to buy their acres, surrender them to other purchasers, or, if lucky, receive pay for the improvements. Land did, in the long run, increase in value, but along an irregular curve instead of an inclined plane. The urge to expand operations in prosperous times resulted in contracts at high prices for land and equipment that could not be retained during the following depression. So the mortgage holders took the profits. When crops brought little, farmers had not the means to buy for speculative holding and therefore were not the ones who gained as times improved. More often, they lost their freeholds and became tenants.

The Agricultural Ladder. There has also been a spate of twaddle about the agricultural ladder, up which hired laborers climbed to tenancy and then to ownership. This actually happened quite often in the seventeenth century, when freed indentured servants found no rigid class lines to hinder their ascent. In 1629 nearly a sixth of the members of the House of Burgesses in Virginia were former redemptioners, and for a few years their percentage increased. But as the slavery system gained power, social lines became harder to cross, and by 1700 opportunity was on the wane. Yet as long as there was a close hinterland into which to retreat, men could still become squatters and reach the status of tenants or freeholders, though always dogged by the more-or-less successful quit-rent collectors. However, the widespread and permanent tenancy on the estates of colonial barons or patroons continued on into the nineteenth century, causing perpetual bickering and occasional violence.

Disposal of the public domain by the federal government in limited parcels at $1.25 an acre after 1820, and the legalization and encouragement of squatting after 1841, came at a time when the frontier had already receded so far that the younger sons of established farmers not remote from the wilderness were the principal ones to seize the advantage. By the time of the Homestead Act of 1862, lands not already monopolized or to be donated to railroad companies were so far distant from centers of population congestion that they were almost unattainable. The great majority of the hopeful claimants of such land soon had to surrender and drift back to places where climate and transportation facilities would permit successful farming. But there the land was so fully occupied that the backwash generally had to seek a livelihood at factory labor. By the end of the nineteenth century the compilers of the Industrial Commission *Report* had to concede that regardless of whatever advantage the agricultural ladder may once have afforded the day laborer or tenant, that device after 1880 was mainly filled by freeholders skidding down into tenancy or work for hire.

By 1900 in the richest agricultural region of the United States, 37.8% of all persons working on farms were wage

laborers making an average of $117 a year; another 19%
were tenants, part-tenants, and managers; while only
43.2% owned or held an equity in their farms. This was
the North Central group of states. The situation was far
worse all over the South. In the more favored section,
724 out of each 1000 farmers received less than $500 a
year and managed to subsist only by the labor of more
than one member of the family. The other 276 ranged
upward from the $500 of tenuous living, but only 84 of
them got the meagerly comfortable income of $1000 or
more. One may imagine the raucous laughter of the
91.6% of all—those constantly aware of their precarious
livelihood—if told that they really were prospering
through the continuous rise in value of their land. They
either did not own it at all, possessed so little that its gain
in value was a mere bagatelle, or were living under the
shadow of the mortgage so frequently commemorated in
the stage plays of the era. Their risibility would be no less
titillated by reminders of the broken-runged agricultural
ladder.

The Farmers' Recourse.    For long periods of time,
and over large areas, there was too little of organized or
concerted revolt against such conditions to warrant any
assumption of the existence of a farmers' movement. It
would require a considerable stretch of imagination so to
designate the early English settlements along the Atlantic
coast; for, among the varied impulses behind that movement, reaction against agricultural submergence in the
old country was negligible. On the other hand, the Scotch-
Irish immigration after 1700 was largely an answer to
English landlordism, and the tendency of the newcomers
to drift out to the frontier was a further symptom of the
desire to remain separated from the detested old connections. Passive resistance in most of the colonies to quitrent
collections was largely an individual matter, but the antirent riots of the nineteenth century were of the essence
of farmers' movements. The plant-cutting episodes of
early Virginia tobacco planters, like the night-rider movement of two centuries later, was an attempt to fix prices;
but Bacon's Rebellion was the outstanding protest against
general abuses in the seventeenth century. One must also
bear in mind that various Indian uprisings, from Opechan-

canough's massacres at least until Black Hawk's Rebellion, were efforts of farmers to maintain their status.

The Revolutionary War, at least as far as it represented an effort to cancel the old tobacco debts and to establish freer access to foreign markets, was definitely an agrarian revolt, though mingled with so many other issues as to exclude it from these pages. But Shays's Rebellion and the Whiskey Insurrection in the following years were of the simon-pure farm-relief variety. The lure of protection for American manufacturers, so as to create a city market for agricultural produce, was a politicians' device that sometimes befuddled the farmers but was not of their creation. The really great farm movement between 1790 and 1860 was a migration to new lands to the westward, best studied in the history of the frontier. The accompanying agitation for free homesteads, though fostered by labor parties and vote-hungry politicians, so caught the rural eye that there is justification for a brief treatment in due order. Even the Civil War was in considerable part the outgrowth of various agricultural strifes, but, like the Revolution, was too complicated with other issues for presentation as a separate movement. The greatest farmers' outbursts came as desirable new lands became scarce and parity declined after 1865. The attempts of rural people to solve these problems, early, intermediate, and late, occupy the following pages.

— 2 —

# REVOLTS OF INDIAN FARMERS

**Opechancanough's Insurrections.**  The first farmers' movements in America were by the Indians. When Opechancanough, head chief of the Powhatans, descended upon the James River settlers in 1644 and slew half a thousand of them, it was the culmination of a long-smoldering resentment against the treatment his people had been receiving from those bleached-out foreigners for a generation or more, and it was his second futile attempt to reverse the trend. These Indians between the James and the York rivers were different in complexion and habits from their newly arrived neighbors, who in consequence looked upon them as savages. Nevertheless, these Indians were a settled people, living in villages and practicing an advanced stage of agricultural economy. They had many hundreds of cleared acres of land on which they grew corn, sometimes a hundred bushels to the acre, in addition to an equal amount of such vegetables as pumpkins, squashes, and beans. For lack of any indigenous animals that could be domesticated for draft purposes, hand implements were the only recourse for cultivation, but for several generations the white man failed to excel these Indians in the quality of produce or the size of crops to the acre.

The Virginia colonists mistreated the natives almost from the start, thus incurring their enmity. John Smith seems to have stood in better esteem with the Powhatans than most Englishmen, but in 1609 he not only bought corn but also sometimes stole 300 or 400 bushels at a time, left two villages destitute of winter food, and seized 300 acres of cleared land near the falls of the James (later Richmond). In 1614, Thomas Dale wrested from the tribe an agreement that for an annual contribution of two and a half bushels of corn from each individual, the English would make no further exactions. This pact held good for eight years. Upon the death of old Powhatan in 1618, his able and less indulgent brother Opechancanough gradually assumed authority over the other chiefs and started planning vengeance. He has been described as calculating and treacherous, but hardly more so than some of the English. Dr. John Pott, the head physician of the Virginia Company, was accused by his own countrymen of killing a considerable number of the Indians by poison.

Opechancanough laid his plans with care and succeeded in lulling the suspicions of Governor Francis Wyatt. Then on March 22, 1622, unarmed Indians entered the homes of the settlers on the pretext of selling game, fish, and fruits. Apparently at a prearranged time about noon, the Indians seized the weapons of their hosts and slew them, man, woman, and child, to the number of 347, and some estimate a still higher figure. Over a quarter of the white population of Virginia fell dead in a short time, and only a partial leak of the plans prevented the slaughter from becoming general throughout the colony. The survivors in the outlying areas, after taking refuge in the few towns, returned and planted their corn and tobacco as usual. Then in the fall they set upon the natives, killing them, burning their villages, and destroying or confiscating their stores of winter food. (*See Document No. 1.*)

This retaliation established relative quiet for several years, but the affair strengthened the British government's charges of gross mismanagement and contributed to the loss of the Virginia Company's charter in 1624. During the next score of years the English confiscation of Indian lands continued, until in 1644 the aged, decrepit, and blind Opechancanough determined to complete his aborted effort of 1622. Striking on April 17, in the ensuing two days his warriors eliminated 500 of their foes. Virginia by this date was so much stronger than at the time of the earlier massacre that panic quickly subsided. Retaliation was swift, protracted, and effective. One Virginia leader after another, culminating with William Claiborne, harried the Indians out of the peninsula clear up to the fall line, destroyed their villages, took over their remaining fields, and broke up the Powhatan confederacy for all time. As a culmination, in 1646 Claiborne ended the war by seizing Opechancanough himself, and three weeks later a vindictive guard killed him by shooting him in the back. Civilization marched on.

**The Pequot War.**   Between these two outbursts, a somewhat similar episode occurred along the lower Connecticut Valley in New England. Here the Pequots, numbering about a thousand warriors, were hemmed in between the Mohegans, partially subject to them, to the west and the Narragansetts to the east. Here, also, Englishmen from Massachusetts Bay were haggling over land purchases with the Mohegans, ignoring the final authority of the Pequots over disposals. As Edward Channing has said, the colonists probably tried to handle the Indians with fairness, "but native intrigues and policies were too involved for their simple English understandings" (*History of the United States*, I, 402). On the other hand, accounts of Indian affairs came only from their white neighbors, and nobody seemed to care about the difficulty the aborigines had in trying to figure out the state of mind of the foreign invaders. This mutual befuddlement began about 1633, developed into individual attacks, and culminated in war in 1637.

In the earlier year the Pequots had killed a Virginia ship captain named Stone and some of his companions, who had seemingly started the trouble. The Boston officials who investigated the affair appeared to accept the theory that Stone himself was responsible, and Governor John Winthrop left it to the governor of Virginia to take any further action. But a year later, when the Pequots asked for an alliance with Massachusetts against threatened encroachments from the Dutch and the Narragansetts, they could get no promise of help except at the cost of a heavy annual tribute for the death of Stone. This form of extortion caused bitterness that flared in intensity when in July, 1636, an agent on his way to collect the current installment of the fine got himself killed by some Narragansett subjects on Block Island, and the Massachusetts authorities blamed the Pequots.

Governor Harry Vane of Massachusetts Bay sent John Endecott with ninety men to kill all Indian men on the island and then turn upon the Pequots on the mainland. The work of bloodshed did not go far, but the burning of Pequot wigwams and cornfields and thefts of stored corn enraged the bewildered and innocent victims of the foray. The authorities both in Plymouth and in Connecticut condemned the action, and the commander of the fort at Saybrook acidly reminded Endecott that he was inviting war. The prophecy came true before the arrival of the following spring. Roger Williams so deftly managed Indian relations that he prevented an alliance between the Narragansetts and the Pequots while the trouble was brewing. The first retaliation against the Endecott invasion occurred when an Indian who could not get payment for land he had sold induced the Pequots to attack Wethersfield, resulting in the death of a few settlers. By May, 1637, when the general court opened at Hartford, the Pequots had slain thirty or more pioneers, sometimes roasting or otherwise torturing them.

The Connecticut authorities then placed about 90 men under John Mason, who was joined by 20 more from Massachusetts under John Underhill (described as "a good fighter, but a sorry scamp") and by some 80 Mohegans and 200 Narragansetts. A Rev. Mr. Stone of Hartford, after laboring all night with the Prince of Peace, emerged with the revelation for a surprise attack on the Indian fort on the Mystic River. The consequence was the most thorough massacre in colonial days. Giving little or no quarter on that early morning of May 20, 1637, the attackers burned the fort and village, cooking or shooting anywhere from 400 to 700 Pequots and capturing seven, while another half dozen escaped. The English losses were two dead and a few wounded by arrows. Mason, then reinforced by 120 men from Massachusetts under Israel Stoughton, overtook another 300 Pequots in a swamp and slew or captured many of them. Their chief Sassacus took refuge with the Mohawks, who sent his head to the English as a token of brotherhood and friendship. Within a short time, the total of slain Pequots mounted to more than 800, while another 200 were sold into slavery in the West Indies and elsewhere. The small remnant scattered and were absorbed among other tribes, and no Pequot nation survived. The various Indian groups, not realizing that they had a common foe, assisted in the elimination of the Pequots, whose farms now became possessions of the English conquerors. Between Stone of Virginia and Stone of Hartford, another movement of natives to preserve their farms was ground to a fine grist. (*See Document No. 2.*)

King Philip's War.   Nearly forty years of quiet followed the extermination of the Pequots. During this time the New England Colonies were growing strong and the Indians were a mere obstacle to further expansion. By 1660 the fur trade was becoming anachronistic in the Yankee economy, and the English no longer felt it worth the trouble to court the red man's friendship. The Puritans had rewarded the kindness of Massasoit by selling off the lands of his Wampanoags, or Pokanokets, and crowding them into the little peninsula of Mount Hope, or Bristol, in Narragansett Bay. Their hunting grounds were gone, their fisheries spoiled, and furthermore, they resented John Eliot's efforts to Christianize them as an additional scheme to weaken them. Refusing to become imitation Englishmen, they roused the government at Plymouth to suspicions of conspiracy. Two years after the death of Massasoit in 1660, his son Alexander also died at Plymouth, where he had been haled to answer accusations of nonexistent plots among the dazed and bewildered tribes. Then Massasoit's other son Meatocom, or Philip as the English renamed him, took charge, harboring deep resentment against what he erroneously assumed was the poisoning of his brother.

During the next twelve years, Philip suffered repeated indignities through forced visits to Plymouth to placate his inquisitors, who invariably treated him as a smooth, oily, and unreliable witness. Such treatment inevitably generated in the Indian minds the very reaction the English had been fearing. Disaffection among the various tribes spread all the way from the Narragansetts and Wampanoags in Rhode Island to the Nipmucks in Connecticut and Massachusetts, and on northward to the Piscataqua River on the border of Maine. Then in 1674 an Indian gossipmonger carried tales to Plymouth, leading to another court session for the haughty Philip. Angry tribesmen thereupon murdered the informer and were hanged for it in June, 1675. Immediately afterward, on June 24, some Wampanoags slew eight or nine Englishmen at Swansea, and Philip had a war on his hands that he did not covet.

Immediately the movement spread to the Nipmucks, who raided Deerfield, Northfield, Springfield, Hatfield, and the surrounding cornfields. Fearing that the Narragansetts would also enter the conflict, Massachusetts, Plymouth, and Connecticut joined forces. Within a few days they drove the Wampanoags out of Mount Hope, and shortly afterward Philip took refuge with the Nipmucks. Canonchet, chief of the Narragansetts, remembering the savage treatment of his father by the English, would not join them, so the white allies captured his fort in the swamps near South Kingston on December 19, 1675, and after heavy losses on both sides, scattered the tribe. Canonchet fell in April, 1676, and in the following month

130 of his followers were mowed down on the banks of the Connecticut River. On August 12, Philip, who had slipped back to Mount Hope, was overtaken by Colonel Benjamin Church, one of whose Indian followers shot the Indian king. The victors sent his hands to Boston and his head to Plymouth, where there was much rejoicing, celebration, and thanksgiving among the Christian colonists.

The tribesmen, without unity or organization, with few arms, scanty supplies, and no hope, had taken up the conflict because they knew no way out of it. With all the savagery in their nature they destroyed about a dozen of the eighty or ninety New England towns, and did heavy damage to half or two thirds of them all. But the outcome was a foregone conclusion from the beginning. It was a heavy blow to the English, who were long in recovering, but it was death to the aspirations of the Indians. Only as allies of the French in the following century did the tribesmen cause further trouble, except that along the border of Maine there were occasional outbursts until the summer of 1678. There, prudence being the better part of valor, the English purchased an amicable settlement of the disputes. This was a precedent which, if it had been more consistently followed than it was, might have been valuable in race relations during the following two centuries. (*See Document No. 3.*)

**Later Indian Troubles.** In all of these Indian uprisings, the central fact is that native farmers were trying to put a stop to white encroachments and to restore an earlier and higher status. The same, in large part, can be said for many later outbursts. What have generally been known as the Conspiracy of Pontiac, Lord Dunmore's War, the Seminole War, and Black Hawk's War, as well as the protracted conflicts in the Old Northwest Territory from 1789 to 1814, were also essentially such farmers' movements. It matters not that guilt was often divided between the opposing forces, that the Indians had other interests than farming alone, or that their objectives may sometimes have been obscure. If one insists on singleness of occupation, aim, and purpose, he would have to rule out all agricultural unrest and omit this book from the series. On the other hand, as the Indian conflicts moved out into the farther West, particularly after 1865, the slighter interest of the aborigines in dirt farming, and the greater reliance on hunting, can justify a reclassification of the troubles, though the same design to restore a *status quo* lay at the bottom of all the movements.

— 3 —

# MOVEMENTS OF COLONISTS

**Opposition to Quitrents.** Though hostility to quit-rents was chronic wherever agents of the king or of pro-prietors attempted to enforce them, the opposition was generally passive and without organization; but occa-sionally there was violence, sometimes protracted. Quit-rents were a vestige of feudalism—annual fees paid by freeholders or copyholders of land to their feudal supe-riors, in lieu of personal services and presumably in return for protection. In effect, the land belonged to the peasant, who could will it to his descendants or sell it on payment of certain penalties. Yet the owners and their heirs from generation to generation had to deliver the pay-ments each year simply because in some remote age a neighboring baron had had power enough to reduce free-holders to the status of dependent villeins. This system prevailed in England only for the reason that it was old and therefore seemed inevitable. But in the colonies, where backwoodsmen were fashioning a different mode of life under new conditions, the imposition did not sit well.

Because of the greater abundance of land, the nearness of a frontier inviting squatters, and the rivalry between colonies in efforts to attract settlers, the rates in America were smaller than those in England. Southward from New York the fees usually ran from two to four shillings a hundred acres, which might seem a rather modest sum. But the more common rate of four shillings equaled a week's wages in the seventeenth century and at least three days' wages on the eve of the Revolution. On rare occasions these rents were somewhat in lieu of additional taxes, but more often they were superimposed upon all taxes. They were paid not by tenants, but by actual landowners, often to persons living overseas whose only relation to the land was the grant of royal favor, and for strangely occult reasons. As annoying as anything else was the knowledge that holders of huge estates often paid only a token quitrent—a beaver skin annually from a New York estate of approximately a million acres or a red rose from one of the greatest landowners of Pennsylvania— while the small farmer was constantly dogged by the collector for his four shillings.

Though the Council for New England had an initial right to collect quitrents, when the title to the land devolved on Plymouth and Massachusetts Bay in 1629, the collections crumbled there and soon lapsed in all the surrounding settlements. All remnants of the system vanished by legislation of 1650. Edmund Andros made a futile effort to renew the practice between 1686 and 1689, and thereafter the nuisance lay dormant and was not resuscitated. The settlement of many New Englanders in East Jersey seems to have had much to do with trouble in rent collections. Efforts by Governor Philip Carteret in 1670 led to utter confusion for a year or two, and at all times there was constant bickering. With the passage of years, most of the proprietors in West Jersey did not care to go to the bother and expense of making collections. In East Jersey in 1744 and later, efforts to enforce the exactions led to a decade of intermittent rioting, sometimes assuming the proportions of civil war. Squatters, lessees, and persons in arrears on their quitrents were numerous enough to control the colonial assembly for several years.

The problem also bedeviled William Penn during the late years of his life, and his descendants after him. Until his death (1718) the rate had been only a shilling for each hundred acres, and favored individuals could escape by payment of a pepper corn, a buck's foot, or an Indian arrow, or the rose before-mentioned. Penn's reply to accusations of being a tyrannical landlord was that he spent more money on the colony than he collected and that his

obstreperous settlers would not pay up. He got so tired
of it all that he wanted to sell out to the king, whereupon
the Pennsylvania legislature accused him of looting the
people and then trying to escape with a capital profit.
From 1719 to 1732 the rate was two shillings, then four,
and after 1768 eight shillings, but there is no record that
the periodical doubling of the rates brought increased
returns. In 1702, James Logan, Penn's agent, reported
that his utmost efforts procured only 3,000 pounds of
flour from all Bucks County. No complete rent roll existed
until 1742. Even when it did, the legislature often re-
frained from assessing the dues. In the back country the
Scotch-Irish resisted manfully, violently, and successfully,
while the courts sided with the farmers. The only safe conclusion is that throughout the colonial period the proprietors did not collect enough to pay them for their efforts.
(*See Document No. 4.*)

In all the rest of the colonies, such rents as were collected came only after serious friction, and there was
trouble everywhere. In Maryland the money went to the
proprietors, and in Virginia and the Carolinas, except in
some proprietory strips, to the king. The returns in
Maryland were somewhat more consistent than to the
southward, but there was constant dispute between the
governors, representing the proprietors, and the assembly,
speaking for the farmers. In Virginia the payments were
in tobacco, usually rated for quitrent purposes at at least
twice the market value and of the poorest grades when
surrendered at all. The king disposed of it at auction.
Collections in the Carolinas were negligible. In North
Carolina the governor's salary came from this source, and
often he received little. With the Revolution, the nuisance
was abated everywhere except on some manorial estates
in New York and in a few isolated spots, particularly in
Pennsylvania, where reverence for obsolete and anachronistic formulas supplanted common sense in a ceremonial
tendering of token payments.

**The Scotch-Irish.** The opposition of the Scotch-
Irish to quitrents suggests the need of a brief account of
the role of this ethnic group in agrarian dissent. Trans-
planted from Scotland to Ulster shortly after 1600, they
soon transformed their new homeland, which had fewer
natural advantages than could be found in Munster, Lein-

ster, or Connaught, into the most prosperous section of Ireland. Within a generation or two, irritated by the tactics of English landlords, some of them began drifting over to America. They had made some settlements in New England as early as 1652, but these early arrivals, like those who came later, did not relish the brand of Puritanism practiced by their English neighbors, preferring the New England frontier to the established settlements. In 1683, others along the eastern shore of Maryland and Virginia organized the first Presbyterian churches in America. Around the year 1700 and afterward, conditions in Ulster became intolerable—perhaps better than in the rest of Ireland, but the Scotch-Irish were not as yet beaten down to the status of submission of their neighbors to the south. Following restrictions on the exportation of livestock, in 1699 the British Parliament, in an effort to stifle the flourishing textile industries of Ulster, passed the Woolens Act prohibiting the exportation of cloth. This in time drove many more expatriates to the American shores, embittered against the English.

In 1704 the imposition of the test oath, as harsh against Presbyterians as against Catholics, caused further dissidence. But by far the greatest stimulus to the exodus was stupid restrictions on tillage and the insatiable extortions of rents by English landlords. Between 1714 and 1718, on the expiration of old leases the rents were doubled and tripled. Wholesale evictions ensued in the County of Antrim, whereupon within two years 30,000 of the dispossessed, distressed, or disgruntled left for America. A new extension of religious toleration then temporarily checked the emigration, but it began again in 1728, and from then to 1750 an average of 12,000 a year crossed the Atlantic. In 1700 there had been more than a million Presbyterians in Ulster, but before the century expired the numbers were hardly half as many. The Anglican Archbishop of Dublin was quick to remind the English (in 1719) that the economic oppression was causing the movement, and the Archbishop of Canterbury took a like view, both probably wanting to play down the matter of religious intolerance and apparently with sufficient justification.

The immigrants came into every colony, but especially Pennsylvania, with New York probably second, and a considerable stream into South Carolina. In New York they built up the agriculture of Ulster and Orange counties. In Pennsylvania they flocked to the frontier areas, where they bore the brunt of Indian hostility, resisted the quitrent collectors, and gave the Quaker aristocracy plenty to worry about. By 1729 James Logan expressed fear that they would become the proprietors of the colony. They became almost as numerous as the Germans who were arriving during the same years but whose persecutions in the old country—political, religious, and economic—were so manifold that their migration was not so clearly a farmers' movement as that of the Scotch-Irish. So grievous had been the experience of the Germans in their homeland that they could be complacent about landlordism in the new land, where they settled down and remained in compact communities. But the Scotch-Irish saw too much of the old British domination, so they continued to spread out to new settlements as far as possible from the old influences. For generations they took the lead in the frontier movement, whether in Maine and Vermont, in the mountain valleys—one stream coming out of Pennsylvania and another from South Carolina—or into the transmontane settlements of Tennessee, Kentucky, and westward.

A considerable number of the Scotch-Irish remained in the seaboard states, sternly upholding their principles. In New Jersey they took the lead in founding what was to become Princeton University. In Virginia they fought to a standstill the Anglican efforts to enforce conformity, and secured some sort of tolerance. In gratitude to James Madison for support in this contest, they later came to his aid in the narrow vote ratifying the Federal Constitution in that state. Memories of bitterness against the English made them the backbone of the frontier adherence to the movement for independence, all the way from Pennsylvania southward. In Pennsylvania it was they who turned the tide for the cause of freedom in 1776, but their hostility to the financial control of the Philadelphia interests put them in opposition to the ratification of the Constitution. Their leadership in later national activities is exemplified by the fact that at least eight of the first seventeen Presidents of the United States were either of Scotch-Irish or Scotch extraction, and there were more to follow before the strain became so thin as to lose significance.

**Bacon's Rebellion.** Resistance to quitrents and the persistent opposition of the Scotch-Irish to British interference with their liberties pale in dramatic effect beside the uprising of Virginia farmers at the same time that King Philip was creating consternation in New England. After about 1638, with the waning of the lush prosperity of the early years of tobacco culture, there was a succession of waves of depressed prices when it hardly paid to grow the weed. Prices ranged from a farthing to fivepence a pound, the general trend being one or two pennies. Production was inelastic and did not readily adjust to correspond with price changes. Much tobacco was produced by small farmers in the backwoods, who raised it as a crop supplementary to mixed farming so as to provide a little ready cash. Even when prices were at the lowest, production continued as long as any money at all rolled in. Great planters also extended their efforts in depression periods, in hope of getting more money or credit.

Whether justifiably or not, tobacco growers felt that the Navigation Act of 1660, placing their staple on the list of goods that could be exported only to England, added measurably to their woes. Direct sales to continental Europe, without this favor to English merchants, might add to profits in Virginia. Starvation and ruin, the planters thought, was their only prospect. This was an exaggerated notion, but hard times were upon them, and this giving to merchants in England the gains from redistribution on the continent was as good a whipping boy as any. A far more real grievance was Charles II's habit of making huge grants of land to his impecunious and profligate toadies, utterly disregarding the prior claims of existing settlers who had what they deemed good title to the soil, but who had to move on or else become subjects of the king's favorites. Furthermore, Governor William Berkeley would not protect the frontier settlements against the forays and depredations of Indians who were taking vengeance on the handiest white men for Berkeley's own bad management of race relations. Even if the governor was not guilty, as charged, of thinking more of his profits from the fur trade than of the safety of the outlying farmers, his actions lent color to the accusation.

On the other hand, in 1660 Berkeley attempted to get a

repeal of the enumeration of tobacco in the Navigation
Law and, failing in this, encouraged the House of Burgesses (the assembly) to pass a law limiting the planting
of tobacco, this "stint," as it was called, to go into effect
only if Maryland also would agree. During the next four
years Virginia continuously repeated this effort to lessen
"the great quantities [of tobacco] now made, w^{ch} glutt all
marketts. . . ." In each case, there was either interference
from England or refusal of cooperation from the Calverts
of Maryland. Meanwhile, tobacco prices remained low,
and poverty spread throughout Virginia. Discontent among
the yeomen developed into bitterness against the colonial
officials. The small farmers had no voice in the government, yet paid most of the taxes, which went for fine
residences in Jamestown and Indian forts so placed as to
afford no protection to the frontier. Berkeley's henchmen
held the large estates, while the bulk of the farmers could
not clear their debts. Sentiment did not improve when in
1673 Charles II gave all of Virginia as a proprietary grant,
presumptively for thirty-one years, to Thomas Culpeper
and Henry Bennett, Duke of Arlington, and in 1675 and
1676 added to the steadily increasing tax rates at a time
of extreme distress and discontent. Furthermore, Governor
Berkeley, who had held office during all the turbulence in
England from 1642 to 1660, retained his position with the
restoration of Charles II, and had not called an election
for a new assembly in sixteen years.

Following a series of Indian troubles, the climax came
in January, 1676, when the Susquehannocks slaughtered
thirty-six English colonists and Berkeley would do nothing
to interfere with the assailants. When in March the assembly met and showed as much incompetence as Berkeley
himself, the people of Charles City County recruited their
own force of 300 volunteers, placing the young Nathaniel
Bacon, only three years out of England, in charge. With
no commission from the government, Bacon set out on his
punitive mission, but all except sixty of his men turned
back when Berkeley proclaimed them rebels and pursued
them with his own little army. Bacon, with his diminished
force, attacked an Indian palisade and slew 150, while
Berkeley had to give up pursuit because of an insurrection
among the citizens and neighbors of Jamestown. The new
rebels compelled the governor to call for the election of a

new assembly and to pardon Bacon, whom Berkeley made a member of his council so as to prevent him from taking the leadership of the legislators. Bacon, fearing treachery, demanded an army commission to lead a force against the Indians, and the council joined with the assembly in enforcing the demand. Bacon's mistrust proved well founded as soon as he headed his 500 men on this second expedition to the frontier. Berkeley immediately rounded up an army, again proclaimed Bacon a rebel, and set out against him. But deserted by his troops and denounced by the bulk of the population of Virginia, the governor had to flee across the bay for refuge in Accomac County, where he found no welcome among the sternest supporters of the king. The whole county, with the exception of a few of the greatest planters, were united behind Bacon.

The rebel chief then really earned the title. Turning back from his campaign, he took control of Jamestown and called a new meeting of the assembly for early September, then returned to his frontier charge. Berkeley now slipped back into the capital with such supporters as he could still command, whereupon Bacon returned again, chased Berkeley back to Accomac, and burned Jamestown on September 19, 1676, so "that the rogues should harbor there no more." Bacon then retired to Gloucester County, where he died on October 26, apparently of swamp fever, though there were ugly rumors of treachery and poisoning. He had barely reached the age of twenty-nine. His popular movement quickly collapsed for want of an effective leader, and by January, 1677, Berkeley was again in control, bent on vengeance. Though the assembly had granted pardon for all treasons and Charles II had proclaimed amnesty, Berkeley promptly hanged twenty-three of the leaders, including William Drummond, who had once been governor of Albemarle. Drummond died within four hours after his capture. In disgust at this display of vengeance, the king declared: "That old fool has hanged more men in that naked wilderness than I have done for the murder of my father." Recalled from his office and in disgrace, Berkeley returned to England, where he died only a few months after Bacon; but it would be asking too much of credulity to accept the report that he died "of a broken heart."

Bacon may have been something of a demagogue, and

his loyalty to the king has been seriously questioned; but there is no doubt about the solid support he got from the beleaguered farmers of Virginia. Even with the rebellion suppressed, a few gains were retained by order of the king, but there were no long-range advantages. Berkeley, with all of his pettifogging ways, was more interested in the welfare of Virginia than were his successors. As to the burning of Jamestown, the fact that nobody cared to rebuild it in its exposed and unhealthful surroundings suggests that Bacon's final display of force was of no serious consequence to the colony. A commission appointed by the king admitted the justice of some of the complaints of the rebels, but of more importance was its restoration of peace with the Indians. (*See Document No. 5.*)

**Plant-Cutting Riots in Virginia.** After the suppression of Bacon's movement, the Royalists held complete sway during the remainder of the century, and the governors were free to oppress and rob the people without hindrance. The reforms adopted in 1676 were soon repealed, and a new charter of government was no improvement over the old one. It granted the assembly no authority over taxation and expressed no guarantees of the king's intention to use discretion in land grants. As Reuben Gold Thwaites has said (*The Colonies,* 1890, p. 80): "These closing years of the seventeenth century were sorry times for Virginia. Riots and consequent imprisonments and hangings were ordinary events. . . . The people were discontented, the province grew poorer as each new governor introduced some fresh extortion, immigration practically ceased, and the spirit of political independence was torpid." Not only was there hostility to the governors, particularly Thomas Culpeper, Francis Howard (Baron of Effingham), and Francis Nicholson, but also against the great planters who dominated the governors' councils, held the best of the offices, and controlled local political affairs. Before 1675 the king had deprived Arlington and Culpeper of their proprietary monopoly, but his demand that quitrents be paid in money instead of overvalued tobacco could not be enforced. Meanwhile Culpeper in four years (1680-1684) saw mainly to the lining of his pockets and then, as Edmund Burke said, returned to England to enjoy "the ample

revenues of his office." Before him, Henry Chicheley had
been utterly ineffective, being described as "superan-
nuated" and as "very sickly, old, and crazy."

During these years, tobacco prices remained distress-
ingly low. Merchants had a large carryover from 1679,
and a huge crop in 1680 so added to the surplus that
there would be enough to supply the demand for two
years even with no planting in 1681. Some estimated that
enough was stored in England to last for five years. Even
Culpeper could not accept this situation with equanimity,
for he could not grow rich from penniless farmers. The
assembly tried to soothe the irate public by limiting the
exportation of tobacco to stipulated ports, which simply
made the local congestion worse and prices lower. The
failure of new efforts to get Maryland to join in crop
limitation made unilateral legislation in Virginia futile, so
no law was passed. Instead, there was drastic action. In
the spring of 1682, first in Gloucester County, gangs of
vigilantes went about from one tobacco patch to another
cutting down as many tobacco plants in an hour's time as
twenty men had counted on for an annual crop. The
movement soon spread into Middlesex and New Kent
counties, and the militia were powerless to suppress it.
The secret bands soon had recruits from servants and
from large planters themselves. They gave up stealth by
night, going boldly about in broad daylight. Let the militia
arrest the men, and the women took over. During the
spring and summer they reduced the prospective crop by
an estimated 10,000 hogsheads (maximum 1000 pounds
each), the product of 5000 laborers for the season.

During these disturbances, Culpeper had been skulking
in England, while his deputy, Chicheley, bewailed the
situation. Against his will Culpeper returned. He ordered
more arrests, but on the whole acted with prudence as
well as energy. Then, the Indians remaining quiet and the
price of tobacco beginning to rise, the plant-cutting
remedy remained unused for some years. But as usual,
there was no permanent organization to keep up the
farmers' determination, and only desperation would bring
action. By 1688 Virginia seemed on the verge of another
revolt, when the overthrow of James II in England led to
Governor Howard's quitting the colony, and vigilance
again relapsed. Thereafter for many years, tobacco prices

fluctuated and there were numerous efforts at legal restriction of production. In 1732 there was a new series of plant-cutting riots, this time in Maryland and neighboring parts of Virginia, which evoked legislation for severe penalties for such activities. The frequent repassage of such laws indicates that the spirit of upheaval was fairly continuous in its vigor. A close and comprehensive farm organization, such as never arrived voluntarily even in later centuries, would have been needed to adjust output to market conditions. Sporadic outbursts at best could effect only temporary amelioration of conditions.

**The Regulator Movement in North Carolina.** Another farmers' uprising, at the very end of the colonial period, calls for brief mention, not because the grievances were unique but because the consequences were more than usually spectacular. The back country of North Carolina was separated from the coastal area by a broad expanse of pine lands of such infertile soil that farmers would not occupy it. Thus the frontier was pretty effectually isolated from the more prosperous plantation regions whose people dominated the government. Between 1767 and 1771 a veritable peasants' revolt occurred in the back counties against economic burdens imposed by corrupt officials. There was scant self-government anywhere in the colony, and least of all in this remote portion, where the population suffered from unbearable taxes, thieving sheriffs, grasping lawyers, and extortionate fees sanctioned by law and enforced by the courts. The scarcity of money made the situation all the more serious.

Taxes were the same for all free people, on the poll basis. They were easily paid by the eastern slaveowners, but were excessively burdensome on the frontiersman who depended almost solely on barter and rarely had any ready cash. When the sheriff arrived without notice to collect the tax, he would refuse to wait until the farmer could visit the neighboring moneylender, but seized some of the property instead, charging 2 s. 8 d. for the service. When the farmer returned with the money, the sheriff, following a route other than his promised one, could not be overtaken until he had disposed of the assets at a neat profit for himself. Governor William Tryon, who was in nowise sympathetic with the back-countrymen, expressed the opinion in 1767 that the sheriffs embezzled over half

of all they collected. For the year 1770 alone they were in
arrears to the extent of £15,000, all coming out of the
farmers' borrowed funds. The matter of fees was another
serious grievance. The fees for lawyers and officials alike
were set by law, and by splitting a service into parts,
several fees often took the place of one. To settle disputes
over such matters, the farmers had to travel as far as sixty
miles to the nearest court, only to find the case postponed
and the costs piling up.

Tryon sided with the officials and would take no action
to correct the situation. Consequently, there was some
mob violence in 1765, a widespread refusal to pay taxes in
1766, and the major Regulator movement in 1768-1771.
During that time the Regulators went on a tax strike,
assaulted sheriffs, lawyers, and judges, and broke up the
court session in Hillsboro. The colonial assembly then
took action, even expelling a duly elected Regulator from
the body. After a long failure to settle the dispute by
negotiation, Tryon met the rebels in the Battle of the
Alamance at the headwaters of the Cape Fear River in
May, 1771, where his army slew some 200 of the farmers.
Six more had inflicted on them the British sentence for
treason which, when carried out literally, comprised
hanging by the neck, being cut down while still living, and
disembowelment, the entrails being burned before the
victim's eyes, which by that time were no doubt sightless,
being beheaded and the body quartered and left at the
disposal of the king, with the pious conclusion, "the Lord
have mercy on your soul." (*See Document No. 6.*)

The people, having failed miserably, had either to eat
humble pie or move to a more distant region. Many did
the latter. Some left before the battle, and it was estimated
that 1500 departed in the year following, going out to lay
the foundations of the State of Tennessee. Josiah Martin
became the next governor of North Carolina (1771-1775)
and he so sedulously courted the good will of the remaining Regulators that many of them were later found in
the ranks of the Tories during the Revolution. The ruling
class and the leaders of the militia had been their enemies.
When these oppressors supported independence, it seemed
only natural and logical to the victims that they should
choose the opposite side.

# MOVEMENTS BETWEEN THE REVOLUTION AND THE CIVIL WAR

**Shays's Rebellion.** The shortage of money exemplified in the Regulator movement was widespread and almost perpetual throughout the colonial period. Then, during the Revolutionary War, with the restraining hand of England removed, the state legislatures as well as the Continental Congress issued such excessive amounts of fiat paper currency as to drive its purchasing value down to nothing by the time of the restoration of peace. The seemingly fantastic prices of produce during those years impelled farmers to expand their operations on credit, and after the war they were faced with the insurmountable task of paying their debts when there was almost no money and their crops were a drug on the market. Foreclosure and prolonged residence in debtors' prisons seemed their only prospect. On the farthermost frontier, where lack of transportation facilities compelled an almost purely self-sufficing economy, the situation was not quite so bad. Less remote areas, such as the interior and western portions of Massachusetts, suffered the worst.

The situation became so bad that in 1786 the soft-money men, not all of whom had the purest of motives, got control of the legislatures in seven states and passed paper-currency laws. In some instances, as in Pennsylvania, the issuances were moderate and the results were salutary, but in Rhode Island the flood of money resulted in debt repudiation until the courts declared the notes not to be legal tender. Connecticut, Delaware, Maryland, Massachusetts, New Hampshire, and Virginia made no concessions at all. The most distressing results came in Massachusetts. The situation of the returned soldier-farmers was especially galling. Their farms had deteriorated during the war and many of the owners had gone in debt to support their families. Their army pay had been in bonds of diminishing value which would not come due for several years. Many of them were losing their homes and going to prison in lieu of balances still owed. On top of all this, Governor James Bowdoin was trying too rapidly to extinguish the state debt and maintain public credit in a period of depression. The most odious of all levies, a poll tax of $1.75 for the poorest as well as the richest, was the main new source of revenue. Creditors were demanding their pound of flesh, while farmers first lost their cattle and horses and then watched the sheriffs auction off their farms. The courts were flooded with suits and the lawyers were reaping the only profitable crops. Complaint was rife against the high salaries of officials and the excessive cost of litigation. (*See Document No. 7.*)

It was not only the wild and woolly rabble that clamored for reform. The sedate town of Quincy asked for the making of "Land a Tender for all debts at the Price it stood at when the debts were contracted." Its neighbor Braintree joined in this demand and also called for the lowering of official salaries, moving the government out of Boston, taxation only on money on hand, and a legislative curb on the power of lawyers. The western town of Amherst went not as far as this, unless a request for a revision of the state constitution could be so construed. All of the county and town conventions stipulated that only legal measures should be employed to obtain redress. But debates over these resolutions gave food to the ruminations of the hotspurs, and a mob spirit arose. The failure of the legislature, adjourning on July 8, 1786, to take any steps for the relief of needy persons facing foreclosure and eviction had prompted the protests from local governments; and soldiers only recently returned from scenes of bloodshed had few qualms against a renewal of the use of violent remedies. The backbone of the rebellious faction was made up of officers and enlisted men of the Continental Army. Daniel Shays himself had been a captain. He was not a man of towering ability; this was not his rebellion more than that of many others; but he was in charge at the most spectacular moment and his name sticks to the movement.

Following a prolonged silence from the government at Boston after the flood of petitions and resolutions, on August 31, 1786, a mob led by Luke Day broke up the court at Northampton, and a similar action happened at Worcester five days later. Job Shattuck then headed a group of merchants who intimidated the judges against holding court in Concord. Like disorders at Taunton and Great Barrington showed that resistance to foreclosures had spread all over the state. Bowdoin then sent 600 of the militia to prevent disruption of the supreme court sitting at Springfield, but Shays was there with probably a thousand men, who prevented the convening of a grand jury to indict the rebel leaders; and so the court adjourned on September 26 and there was no further session in the western part of the state until March, 1787.

While the insurgents were in Springfield, Governor Bowdoin reconvened the legislature, which passed various acts and resolutions designed to convince the people that the government was operating in an efficient, economical, and reasonable manner, without going very far in the way of concessions. An offer of indemnity to all who would swear allegiance within a given time was coupled with a riot act and a suspension of the writ of habeas corpus. Another law offered lower costs of litigation by extending the list of civil cases that could be tried before justices of the peace, and still another made certain real and personal property legal tender. The legislature also made provision for further use of the militia to end the disorders, but rioting continued. A mob again broke up the court at Worcester, but effective resistance ended in eastern Massachusetts when on November 30 a company of cavalry prevented a new insurrection in Concord and captured Job Shattuck. But Shays continued his activities, gathering a force of some 1200 for final action at Worcester, an attack on Cambridge, and the capture of the United States arsenal at Springfield. Forbidding December weather and the determined stand of Cambridge resulted in a disorderly retreat of the Shaysites westward. (*See Document No. 8.*)

By this time, official apprehension was rampant. Congress authorized General Henry Knox to recruit 1340 men, presumably for action against the Indians but actually for defense of the arsenal at Springfield. These troops, not being needed, were not used. Also, Bowdoin sent General Benjamin Lincoln with a force of 4400 to finish the work already begun by General William Shepherd (or Shepard). The immediate financing of this expeditionary force was by means of loans from frightened merchants anxious to guard their wealth.

At Springfield, Shays was supported by Day and Eli Parsons. Day tried to inform Shays that he could not appear for the assault on the arsenal until January 26, 1787, but the interception of this message gave Shays confidence that the attack could take place on the 25th as scheduled. This was also before the arrival of Lincoln, but Shepherd had no difficulty in repelling the Shaysite charge, killing four of the insurgents. Lincoln arrived on the following day and took up the pursuit toward Amherst. Near that destination, Lincoln cut off Luke Day, who took refuge in New Hampshire, while Shays turned back eastward. Lincoln overtook the fugitives at Petersham on February 4, capturing 150 and dispersing the rest, while Shays himself fled into Vermont. Before the end of the month, everything was quiet. In March, the legislature pardoned everybody but Shays, Day, and two others. Shays received a death sentence which the succeeding governor remitted on June 13, 1788, and Shays remained in obscurity in New York until his death in 1825.

The lenity of Bowdoin did not save him in the gubernatorial election. He lost in the spring of 1787 to John Hancock, characterized by James Schouler as a man "whose light shone through a horn-lantern of vanity and love of popular applause" (*History of the United States,* 1880, I, 34). This in itself was in part a posthumous vindication of the rebellion, which in other ways also was not a complete fiasco. The legislation immediately afterward reduced court fees, exempted personal effects and tools from seizure for debt, extended the legal-tender law, allowed release of debtors who could not support themselves in jail, and lowered taxes on polls and estates. Of more widespread and lasting effect was the consternation of conservative delegates to the Constitutional Convention that got under way at Philadelphia on May 25, 1787. Their denial to the states of the power to "make any Thing but gold and silver Coin a Tender in Payment of Debts" (Constitution, Art. IV, sec. 10, par. 15), the authority of Congress to call out the militia to "supress

Insurrections" (Art. I, sec. 8, par. 15), and the federal
guarantee to each state of "a Republican form of Government" and executive response to the request of a legislature or governor to protect any state "against domestic
Violence" (Art. IV, sec. 4) can be traced directly to the
panic created by Shays's Rebellion.

**The Whiskey Insurrection.** As Shays's Rebellion
pointed to the need of federal authority over local disturbances beyond the power of the individual states to
handle, so the Whiskey Insurrection of seven years later
demonstrated central power in action. The trouble arose in
southwestern Pennsylvania, and particularly in Washington, Allegheny, Fayette, and Westmoreland counties,
a region largely occupied by the Scotch-Irish. These
people, as noted in Chapter 3, had not been enthusiastic
about the ratification of the Federal Constitution, and they
were also discontented with parts of the new constitution
of the state. They wanted cheap land, easy money, and
light taxes, in contrast to the opposite interests of the
merchants, financiers, and land monopolists of the eastern
portion of the state. Furthermore, the western farmers
had lost their natural commercial outlet through New
Orleans when Spain closed the Mississippi River to American trade in 1784, an action that the moneyed interests
around Philadelphia condoned because of privileges in
trade that they still retained. On top of this, the government had not yet done anything effective toward the
settlement of the Indian troubles in the Old Northwest,
which also menaced the future of frontier Pennsylvania.
As a crowning grievance came Alexander Hamilton's
excise law of March, 1791, placing a tax of from 9 to 25
cents a gallon on whiskey.

Such an impost was not new in Pennsylvania, having
been known since 1684, but it had been easily evaded
and rarely had there been a serious effort to enforce or
collect it. A particularly odious feature of the new act was
the provision for periodical inspection of all stills, search
of households for hidden liquor, and payment in specie
on the spot. These farmers had no easy access to the
East, as the New Yorkers had by way of the Mohawk
River, but the flatboat trade down the Ohio and Mississippi rivers before 1784 had encouraged more interest in
commercial farming than could be found on the frontier

to the southward. The hauling of rye and corn to the Atlantic coast was out of the question in that period when roads were merely trails. But two kegs of whiskey could be suspended from the back of each pack horse in a train and carried to Cumberland, Hagerstown, or Baltimore, where whiskey worth 50 cents a gallon along the Monongahela River would easily bring twice that price. Thus was found a way to market the corn and rye and bring in a little of the much-needed specie, which was soon spent.

Farmers distilling only moderate amounts of whiskey had not the money on hand to pay the tax at the still; otherwise, they could simply have included the excise as an added cost to be recovered at a profit on sale. Thus, many of them were faced with the prospect of abandoning their only source of money income, to the advantage of capitalistic distillers who were already beginning to expand and who had reserves on hand to satisfy the collectors of revenue. Why, the small farmer argued, should he raise the money the government required to pay interest to bond speculators and wartime profiteers? Lament of this sort extended throughout the back country everywhere until, late in 1792, Congress exempted the smallest stills—those doing only a neighborhood business in table and medical supplies—from the exaction. This ended discontent south of Pennsylvania, but in Pennsylvania itself nearly all of the stills were large enough to remain taxable. To cap the climax, the amendment contained a loophole —the tax being levied on the basis of the annual capacity of the still—which made the cost to the capitalistic enterprisers, who operated the year round, far less a gallon than would have to be paid by the farmer, whose stills were cool during much of the year.

Faced with the necessity of abandoning the business to a whiskey monopoly and reverting to a purely self-sufficient agricultural life, the farmers refused to pay and began threatening the inspectors. There were about 5000 operators in the business, and united they could be a formidable antagonist. During 1792 and 1793 they contented themselves with refusing to register their stills and smashing those of timid souls who complied, sometimes injuring the owners as well. Bills signed by "Tom the Tinker" were posted in conspicuous places, warning the complacent and submissive. (*See Document No. 9.*) In

1792 Hamilton induced President George Washington to issue a proclamation of warning, to which the farmers paid no attention. Any violation of the law made the culprit liable to trial in the federal courts, and there was none closer that Philadelphia, at least 350 miles distant. This situation was so preposterous that in June, 1794, a new law provided for trials in state courts for defendants living more than fifty miles from a federal court. But this was not in time to prevent violent reaction against old warrants in the following month.

For three years the noisiest leader of the excise opponents had been David Bradford, the prosecuting attorney of Washington County, while Albert Gallatin of the same county, though sympathetic, headed the forces for moderation. H. H. Brackenridge, more cautious than Bradford and in whose favor much can be said, was another leader of the more strenuous opposition to the tax. Whether Bradford's support came from the Democratic societies in Washington County is uncertain, but where those groups flourished, there hostility to the excise was most intense. After annual sessions of irate farmers in 1791 and the following years had advocated violation of the law, in July of 1794 a federal marshal appeared in the neighborhood of Pittsburgh with fifty old warrants summoning objectors to appear before the federal court in Philadelphia. The contest now entered its acute stage. A group of insurrectionists prevented the marshal and the inspector, John Neville, from serving the writs, and on the following day, July 16, they burned Neville's house after his men had killed one and wounded six of the assailants. By this time, there were 600 insurgents in arms, and Neville had to flee for his life.

Bradford then tried to generate a full-fledged revolt, binding the whole population to the support of those who had expelled Neville. A preliminary session at the Mingo Creek meetinghouse arranged for a great mass meeting at Parkinson's Ferry (on the Monongahela River in Washington County) on August 14. Then, by robbing the mails, Bradford got hold of some letters from Pittsburgh citizens who were hostile to his movement, appealing for help from the East. Publication of these letters brought further solidarity in the four counties. Then Bradford assembled between 5000 and 7000 of the local militia on Braddock's

Field on August 1. Some of them went along just to restrain the effervescence of others, but at least 2000 of the men bearing arms were determined to raid Pittsburgh and drive out some of their opponents. This campaign proved a farce when the hospitable Pittsburghers plied the militia heavily with whiskey, one citizen declaring that he alone contributed 400 gallons of rare old liquor.

In view of the insurrectionary activity of the western militia, Governor Thomas Mifflin of Pennsylvania was reluctant to call out even those from the rest of the state, lest they fraternize with the militiamen in revolt. But President Washington was not thus restrained. On August 7 he sent out a new proclamation against the rebels and called 15,000 militia from Pennsylvania and the neighboring states of New Jersey, Maryland, and Virginia, to set out for the West on September 1. Washington and Mifflin also each appointed a few commissioners to confer with the troubled farmers at their Parkinson's Ferry confabulation on August 14. Here, 220 delegates assembled from the four Pennsylvania counties and 6 more from Ohio County in the northern panhandle of (West) Virginia. Gallatin was able to hold the malcontents in partial restraint against the allurements of Bradford, but many remained obdurate. The rest of August and all of September brought no settlement of the differences. Before the end of this time the commissioners, convinced that the inspection law could not be enforced, returned to Philadelphia and so informed Washington and Mifflin. On September 25 the President issued a new proclamation against those who remained recalcitrant and ordered a concentration of the militia. Bradford, hearing that the army was on the march, was the first to flee, and he did not stop until he reached New Orleans.

The call for so huge a force—more men than Washington had ever commanded alone during the Revolution and more than the number of men of military age in all the disaffected region—was Hamilton's idea. A thousand men would have been more than an ample force. But Hamilton was apparently suffering with delusions of military grandeur and insisted on accompanying the men, who were under the command of Henry (Light Horse Harry) Lee, all the way to the scene of the trouble. Washington, caught in a moment of weakness of judgment, acceded and also went along as far as Bedford, two thirds of the total distance, where he had to turn back to be in Philadelphia when Congress convened. Faced with open warfare against insuperable odds, on October 2 the farmers reassembled at Parkinson's Ferry and transmitted a message of submission to Washington, who by that time had reached Carlisle. But the two columns of the army, one following John Forbes's earlier route and the other along the Braddock Road, kept advancing and on November 8 converged on Parkinson's Ferry, where a third session of the convention had assembled to meet them.

There, Lee granted amnesty to all who took the oath of allegiance, and Hamilton set about arresting all he could find of those who still held out. Eighteen of these had to go to Philadelphia to stand trial for treason in the following May. John Mitchell and Philip Weigel, the one hardly more than a half-wit and the other obviously insane, were convicted, whereupon some disinterested Philadelphians of philanthropic impulses, realizing that the men were not responsible for their actions, easily induced Washington to pardon them. Lee left 2500 of the militia in the area for the winter, just as a precaution. He had been met at Parkinson's Ferry, not by a wild rabble of armed and angry men, but by an affable if dissatisfied group more than ready to make peace. (*See Document No. 10.*)

Many times since 1794 there has been trouble with illicit distillers, but never until the Prohibition Era with such a tight-knit organization. The situation in western Pennsylvania soon improved, though not because of the revolt. The presence of the troops for a few months increased the amount of money in circulation. Anthony Wayne's victory over the Indians in the Old Northwest (1794) and the consequent Treaty of Greenville (1795) left the frontier open for a flood of immigrants ready to buy surplus produce. The Pinckney Treaty with Spain (1795) reopened the Mississippi River outlet for grain. Farmers turned to the feeding of their cereals to livestock which they drove over the mountains to market, and distilling no longer was a necessary source of ready cash. While the insurrection gained nothing for the farmers, the manner of its suppression had an adverse effect on the future of the Federalist Party. People did not readily forget what seemed to them an effort to create a military autocracy. So they added this incident to a growing list which a few years later swept the party forever out of power. The "Sons of the Whiskey Rebellion," a distillation of recent years, seems to have imbibed much of the spirit of the movement of 1794, with little if any lineal descent.

**The Antirent Riots in New York.**    After the Whiskey Insurrection, while farmers were moving westward and becoming involved in political disputes over the tariff, federal aid for the development of transportation facilities, banking problems, and the proper means of disposal of the public lands, tenants on the manorial estates of southeastern New York were striving to sunder the bonds of feudalism. As late as 1846 in a huge triangle the corners of which might roughly be marked by the cities of Rome, Troy, and White Plains, there were thirteen counties largely monopolized in huge tracts and leased out for two or three lifetimes, for ninety-nine years, or in perpetuity. This was after seven years of almost continual and partially successful struggles on the part of the tenants to terminate the system.

The origins of these vast holdings go back to the early years of Dutch occupancy, when Kiliaen Van Rensselaer, an Amsterdam gold and diamond merchant and a member of the Dutch West India Company, built up the only successful patroonage, comprising nearly all of Albany and Rensselaer counties and part of Columbia County. It was a tract 24 by 48 miles in dimensions, an area nearly equal to that of Rhode Island. The English later confirmed the grant and defined the quitrent. Kiliaen remained an absentee landlord of Rensselaerwyck, but six of his descendants in order retained control of the manor, letting it out to tenants in perpetual leaseholds, until the death of Stephen Van Rensselaer in 1839. Primogeniture then being illegal in New York, the title went to the two sons, Stephen and William, and at this time the troubles started.

The early English governors far exceeded the Dutch in squandering the public domain on favorites. By 1684 Robert Livingston had secured patent to a tract 10 by 18 miles in area in Columbia County. But the size grew mysteriously, so that in 1702 the reform Governor Richard Coote (Earl of Bellomont) could say: "I am told Livingston has on his great grant of 16 miles long and 24 broad, but four or five cottages, occupied by men too poor to be farmers, but are his vassals." Here was a tract of approximately 2,500,000 acres, the proprietor having all feudal privileges and manorial jurisdiction. It remained in the Livingston family, being divided into four parts in 1792. The manor proper, as distinguished from the entire estate, was calculated in 1715 at 160,240 acres, on which improvements were in rapid progress. During the Revolutionary War and for some years afterward, the tenants disputed the Livingstons' title. Riots and attempted evictions were common events until 1795, when the failure of an effort to break the title resulted in forty years of relative quiet. Governor Benjamin Fletcher (1692-1698) had been so lavish in his distribution of favors that Bellomont (1698-1702) declared three quarters of the best land of the colony had gone to about thirty persons. After a brief respite under his administration, between 1702 and 1708 Governor Edward Hyde (Viscount Cornbury) continued the despoilation, allowing Johannes Hardenberg 2,000,000 acres in Delaware, Ulster, Sullivan, and Greene counties, and large amounts to other individuals and groups. The Great Hardenberg holdings were divided into 42 parts for sale in 1749, and the purchasers themselves became great landlords.

Some proprietors gradually partitioned their manors into farms for cash sales in fee simple absolute, after which there was no controversy. Others sold on long terms, some of the contracts causing difficulties in the western part of the state in 1835 and 1836. It was leasing on the greater estates for a succession of lifetimes or in perpetuity that caused the antirent agitation. The terms of many of the contracts, revealing that the annual payments were at least in part in lieu of feudal services, show that this was simply a continuation of the quitrent problem of colonial days. The quitrents usually ranged between $7 and $18 for each hundred acres. The elder Stephen Van Rensselaer for many years had not bothered to collect the fees from favored tenants or such others as had difficulty in making the payments, and on his death his heirs claimed that $400,000 of arrears were due. But the debts of the deceased totaled almost the same amount, and the sons expected the tenants to make good. The younger Stephen was particularly tactless in refusing to treat with the harassed debtors or to sell any of the land on any terms. Thereupon the leaseholders began forming antirent associations in various parts of the state, determined to resist collection by the Van Rensselaers or any other manorial landlords. Disguised as Indians, and with a military organization, they gave a good account of their constancy for several years.

In the summer and fall of 1839 the sheriff of Albany County made various efforts to serve writs of eviction and of *fieri facias,* but each time bands of farmers and sympathizers, unarmed or armed only with clubs, turned him and his deputies back. On December 2 he had a posse of 500, but again had to retreat when confronted by the superior force of 1800. Governor William H. Seward (1839-1843) was reluctant to use the militia except as a last expedient, but before the end of the month he did so, at the same time appealing to the citizens of the county to refrain from unlawful assemblies but to assist the officers in the performance of their duties. The troops had to remain in the field only three days while the sheriff served all the processes and writs and made all the arrests and levies on property for which he had authorization. Soon afterward, on January 7, 1840, Seward addressed the legislature, deploring feudal tenures and recommending a commission to adjust the differences between tenants and landlords. To this request the legislature complied in May, but negotiations between the Van Rensselaers and their underlings came to nought.

Meanwhile disturbances revived for a couple of years in Albany County and then spread across the Hudson into Rensselaer and Columbia counties. There was incessant interference with the service of writs, while the antirent associations carried on a campaign of publicity in the newspapers and memorialization of the legislature. The official acts of these bands were legal and moderate, but the use of disguises made them chargeable not only for their own misdeeds but also for those of others who had private grudges to settle. In 1844 the activities of masked bands threw Columbia County into an uproar and made the county seat of Hudson into an armed camp. After the murder of two unoffending persons and an assault on the sheriff, a deputy put two antirenters in the Hudson jail, which caused wild talk of opening the prison and burning the town. The trial of the two offenders in December resulted in a hung jury, but a second trial in September, 1845, brought a life sentence for one; the other, accused only of riot and assault and battery, drew two years. The legislature then outlawed masked and armed persons, but neither action ended the disorders.

In May of 1845 the sheriff and one of the two deputies who were ambushed with him suffered serious wounds. Greene, Montgomery, Schoarie, and Delaware counties experienced widespread lawlessness during the ensuing summer. The destruction of papers and the tarring and feathering of deputies were common occurrences. As the culmination of hostilities in Delaware County, one Osman N. Steele, a deputy helping the sheriff to execute a writ of seizure of property for arrears in rent, was killed on August 1. This caused Governor Silas Wright (1845-1847) to declare a state of insurrection in the county and to call out 300 of the militia. Over a hundred arrests followed, and sixty or more other indicted rioters fled. In September, 1845, twenty-eight of the accused were convicted on a series of minor charges and received fines ranging from $20 to $500. Fifteen others drew sentences as low as two years and as high as ten for robbery and manslaughter. Five more got life terms for first-degree manslaughter. Two, convicted of murder in the first degree, were sentenced to hanging, which decree Wright commuted to life sentence. Entering politics, the antirenters elected for governor John Young (1847-1849). He was from Geneseo, in the western part of the state where there was also a discontented tenantry. In January, 1847, he pardoned the eighteen still in prison.

In other ways, also, the antirenters tried to influence state politics. In 1844 they asked the legislature to vacate the faulty Rensselaer title and give to the tenants the farms they operated. The petition was referred to a committee containing some very able antirenters, but the report favored the landlords. This put a stop to organized resistance, but opposition to paying the rents continued and there were occasional killings and other bloodshed for at least forty years following. But most of the landlords, including the Van Rensselaers and the Livingstons, grew weary of the contest and allowed their tenants to buy their farms at reduced prices until only a fragment of the baronial estates remained. Late in 1845, the Van Rensselaer interests reached an agreement with the tenants whereby the latter could buy their land for a sum that at 6% interest would bring the equivalent of the previous rental. This made the average sale price about $2.30 an acre. By 1860, many of the Van Rensselaer farms in Albany County had been purchased on these terms. During the years of greatest strife, the antirenters held the balance of power in the legislature. By bargaining they got some laws discouraging to the leasehold system, and a new state constitution in 1846 prohibited its extension. Governors Seward and Wright had lent encouragement to the changes, and they were assisted by Samuel J. Tilden.

**Influence of the Farmers' Movement Westward.**   Violent movements like that in New York were infrequent in the nineteenth century, except for Indian uprisings such as those of Osceola and Black Hawk which, not vitally different from those of the colonial period, must surrender space to other issues. The mild and political nature of other contests can be attributed in large part to the fact that the Treaty of Paris of 1783 and later territorial expansion made available the best farming lands on the continent even more rapidly than migrating families could occupy them. Benjamin Franklin, looking back over the gradual expansion of the colonial generations, had once opined that several centuries would pass while Americans were settling the eastern Mississippi Valley. The creation of states in all of that territory and ten more to the westward by 1864 is testimony of the lure of this country to the multiplying native-born population and to a large portion of the immigrant horde, in little more than seven decades after the sage's death. Though, as the factory system gained headway, it became increasingly difficult for wage earners to take advantage of the new agricultural opportunities, eastern farm owners, discontented with conditions in their home localities, could generally sell out for enough to finance the move and, thanks to their previous experience, to make a success of it. This left no dent in the eastern labor market, but it did tend to minimize agrarian discontent, even when the competition from western farms upset the farming pattern in the North Atlantic states. By that time the rapidly growing cities furnished a new release for the disgruntled farmers.

**Free-Homestead Agitation.** A growing liberality in the federal land-disposal policies after 1800 contributed to the ease with which agriculturists could acquire new tracts. Even before the Preemption Act of 1841 legalized squatting on the public domain, giving the settlers first right to purchase as much as 160 acres at the minimum price of $1.25 an acre, a movement was under way for free homesteads. This originated in the eastern labor parties of the early Jacksonian movement, as a proposed alleviation of conditions among the industrial workers. At least as early as 1828 it found expression in *The Mechanics' Free Press,* and by 1835 George Henry Evans was evolving a veritable agrarian philosophy that received full expression in his *Working Man's Advocate* in 1844. (*See Document No. 12.*) He would end all selling of public land and would dispose of it in maximum lots of 160 acres to persons who would farm it. Such tracts should remain free of any threat of monopoly control even by seizure for debts. In order that eastern laborers could get their share, the government was to pay for necessary equipment and for transportation to the land, this cost being less than the maintenance of poor relief. This idea gained rapid and wide support, and about a third of the country's newspapers, including Horace Greeley's *Tribune,* were advocating at least a part of the program by 1850.

Since the 1820's Senator Thomas Hart Benton of Missouri had been moving toward somewhat the same position, and western farmers were becoming enthralled with the idea. In 1846 various members of Congress, including Andrew Johnson of Tennessee, introduced homestead bills of a watered-down nature. Down through 1853 the support in Congress for such a measure was almost solely from the states west of the Appalachians, north and south, while the opposition came from the entrenched Atlantic seaboard interests, again both north and south, who wanted to maintain land prices, prevent mobility of labor, and restrain the growth of the bumptious West. When the Republicans began making a political issue of the policy in 1856, and the following years, winning eastern support in return for western concessions to the eastern version of limitation of slavery expansion, the division became one between the North and the South. Before this time, both Hannibal Hamlin, Lincoln's running mate in 1860, and Gerrit Smith the abolitionist had voted against the proposed release of eastern wage slaves.

The diluted measure finally adopted in 1862 was, for a variety of reasons, disappointing in its effects. The proposals of Evans, if fully adopted, might have done much to relieve pressure in the eastern labor market, giving the worker a choice between toiling in the factory or on the farm. But the law as adopted contained none of the provisions he had advocated for getting the laborers to the land and giving them an encouraging start. Consequently, they could not make the move, but had to remain behind with no safety valve against industrial explosions. Even the farmers gained but little. The act came after much of the best of available lands in a climate with adequate rainfall was already cornered by speculators. The law did not put an end to monopolistic grants, but instead was accompanied by a policy that resulted in the donation of a tenth of the area of the United States to railroad corporations. Down to 1890 farmers got an area less than that of the state of Nebraska, while twice as many as those who succeeded had to give up and return eastward. In the same years, the railroads got nearly four times as much as all of the homesteads, to hold for profitable sale. Charles A. Beard, in summarizing researches of the 1930's, accurately pictured the conclusions by saying the Homestead Act was "almost a fraud upon farmers and industrial workers. . . ." (*America in Midpassage*, 1939, p. 552).

**Farmers' Political Attitudes.** On economic issues in politics, the farmers were highly opportunistic, usually dividing along sectional lines. By 1815 the old "War Hawks" of 1812, including Henry Clay and John C. Calhoun, began thinking of themselves as the "Nationalists," advocating a permanently large military force, high tariffs to foster manufactures, centralized banking, and federal aid in the building of a national network of navigable rivers, canals, and roads. By 1820 the infant-industries argument for the tariff beginning to wear thin, Clay started to elaborate the theory of protection of manufactures so as to build up cities as markets for an agricultural surplus produced by a temporary decline in foreign demand that the tariff itself had helped bring on as a reprisal. For a time this home-market argument had a particular appeal to the farmers of the Old Northwest, especially when coupled with the promise of the spending of the surplus revenue thus obtained on internal improvements. The lowered cost of transportation for goods bought or sold would more than offset increased prices of imports and of domestic manufactures.

Thus the West supported the tariff bills of 1824 and 1828, but began to lose enthusiasm when suspicion started hovering over the internal-improvement program. In 1830 Clay's following in Congress passed a bill for federal aid in the building of a road in Kentucky between Maysville, on the Ohio River, and Lexington. Their idea was to discredit President Andrew Jackson. If he accepted the bill, he would lose support in the South, which felt it could take care of its own improvements more cheaply than by participation in a federal program. If he vetoed the measure, he would alienate the Northwest. To the consternation of the backers, however, Jackson's veto brought him increased support from the farmers north of the Ohio. If charity were to begin at home, they preferred it to be at their homes and not at Clay's home at Lexington. From that time until 1860, the Western farmers were rather indifferent on the tariff, though in most periods they have been gullied by protectionist arguments.

For a time the Southern farmers were quite complacent about protection, accepting Calhoun's argument that the rise of Northern factories would create an additional market for cotton. They soon found, however, that John Randolph's position was more to their liking. The expansion of Northern mills had no effect on the world demand for cloth, but the high tariffs added to living costs, and England's reprisals adversely affected the foreign demand for American cotton. Before 1828 Calhoun had to reverse his stand and become a free trader in order to retain his political leadership in South Carolina. The ensuing nullification movement, only a partial victory at the best, was a farmers' response to protective tariffs, an opposition that the South has rather consistently maintained ever since. Farmer reaction on the United States Bank controversy after 1828 was based primarily on economic status. In areas where agriculture was debt-ridden there was opposition to the bank, while large planters and the more prosperous of other farmers in general supported it.

On the question of slavery expansion, there was after 1820 a rather common acceptance by all classes in the East of the theory that no more territories should be opened up to slavery. Thus they would maintain the *status quo* of sectional superiority. The Missouri Compromise line and abstention from further annexation of territory to the southwest would achieve this aim. In the West and in the South, the problem was of primary concern to farmers. Western farmers were concerned with cheap land in the territories for themselves or their sons, where they did not want competition with plantation estates or with Negro labor. They were looking toward Kansas, Nebraska, and Oregon, but had no interest in Texas as a future home. Hence, in 1844 they were ready to bargain with the South and jointly adopt the slogan of "the reoccupation of Oregon and the reannexation of Texas." Political horse trading, as on the homestead question, was before 1860 to merge the East and the West in a common support of the Wilmot idea of total exclusion of slavery from the territories.

The South also had its differences of opinion. The border-state farmers, with surplus slaves to sell, favored extended markets in new slave territories and were opposed to the reopening of the slave trade with Africa. Persons in the lower South who hankered for new opportunities in the West, agreed on expansion but preferred renewed importation of slave labor so as to get it cheaper. Established planters were not anxious for the acquisition of so much new territory, adapted to the plantation system, as to overexpand production and beat down the price of cotton, but they resented Northern agitation to stop this sort of growth. Neither were they enthusiastic for a reopening of the trade in chattels from Africa, lest it should depress the value of the slaves they already owned. Yet there were some of them who, desiring to enlarge operations, felt the opposite way about it. Here were some of the conflicting farmers' issues that with the stimulus of outside interference could result in compromise and consolidation in the South like that going on in the North, and produce civil war. One should, also, not lose sight of the fact that the South, in an inferior economic position largely because the strait jacket of slavery hampered diversified activity, felt more comfortable if it could lay the blame on what it called financial bondage to the North. These suggestions as to underlying motives may help to explain some of the seemingly irrational strife that resulted, but they are no substitute for a more thorough study of the subject.

— 5 —

# POST-BELLUM FARMERS' MOVEMENTS

**Effects of the Civil War.** During the Civil War, the prices of farm products had risen amazingly as measured by the rapidly depreciating greenback dollar. But when the value of the dollar got down to forty cents or less in terms of gold, wheat could sell at twice the price it brought in 1860 and still have a smaller purchasing power. Furthermore, there was some decline in production even of Northern crops, while the South barely managed to subsist. There was one temporary advantage of greenback prices—debts could be paid off with greater ease. But the average farmer, deluded by $2 wheat, was more inclined to speculate for later huge profits, only to find himself inextricably further in debt when the war ended and money again became scarce. Also, the shortage of man power caused by the demands of the army not only put the women, children, and old folks in the field, but lent encouragement to the purchase of all the labor-saving machinery the factories could roll out and that credit could cover at wartime prices—again, to be paid for in later years of low financial returns. Even in the North the war brought a diminution of agricultural wealth.

The effect on the South was worse than that on the North. The planters not only found their labor force disrupted, but their working capital was gone, transportation was broken down, market facilities were deficient, and credit was almost unobtainable. The loss of property in slaves was in itself of minor consequence, for the labor was still obtainable at the cost of sustaining life in the workers. But it took time to regain control, and the system finally evolved was so degrading in its economic and moral effects on the semi-free men as to make them even less efficient than they had previously been as slaves. All of the Confederate money and bonds were worthless, and land values were sometimes as low as only a tenth of the prewar level. By 1870 the average was about half that of a decade earlier. Except in Texas, largely isolated from the rest of the South, the number of livestock was greatly diminished. Buildings were depleted, fences were down, farm implements were worn out, and large areas suffered from the depredations of advancing or retreating armies. By the end of the war, hundreds of thousands of people were destitute, and all feared retribution for the rebellion. Nearly all of the cotton stored for sale after the war had gone for stopping cannon balls, had been burned to prevent seizure by invading forces, had been destroyed by Union raiders, or had been confiscated by the North.

The effect of the extravagance of later carpetbag governments can easily be overstressed. The Southern states ultimately repudiated most of the debts thus piled up, and speculators abroad paid the penalty for lack of caution. The great change in landownership resulting from mortgage sales meant no significant breakup of large estates. In fact, the number of large plantations in proportion to small farms continued to grow, sharecropping, tenancy, and hired labor taking the place of the earlier slave labor. But it was the rural-credit system (to be described presently) that ultimately brought political revolt.

**Farmers' Grievances: Money and Prices.** The farmers' central grievance in the late decades of the nineteenth century was the lack of parity with other economic groups, though they used other terms to describe the situation.

The plain fact was that agriculture was hardly paying for the effort expended on it, and the gap between poverty and plenty seemed to be widening. Low prices for crops and livestock and the high cost of purchased necessities combined with scarce money, tight credit, towering interest rates, burdensome transportation charges, and the exactions of the middlemen—particularly the produce exchanges, grain elevator operators, and meat packers—to make agriculture a doubtful commercial venture and hardly even a way of life. Wealth came from the tilling of the soil, but relatively few actual dirt farmers, except those who were also landlords or were engaged in other exploitative activity, had much better than a hand-to-mouth existence. The shocking status at the end of the century, even in the granary and larder of the nation, was not an exceptional one in time and place.

The scarcity of money for the country as a whole was largely a relative matter. If one could imagine a long-range static demand in all financial transactions, then an unchanging per capita amount of circulating currency and instruments of credit, whether large or small, would maintain stability. But in reality demand is constantly changing, as is also the per capita number of dollars. If fixed obligations, such as mortgages, bonds, contracts, insurance, and the like, were gauged to the purchasing value of the dollar, monetary inflation or deflation would cause little anxiety except to bookkeepers, accountants, and statisticians. But, again, this is thinking in a vacuum. The farmer's trouble was that in an erratically changing economy the supply of money lagged behind demand, his obligations were fairly constant, and his lack of credit deprived him of the supplementary medium of exchange that came to the aid of more favored businesses.

With the return of the Southern states into the economy, even if not yet into the Union, the wartime supply of Northern money had to do business for the whole reunited nation. So, the per capita of money fell from $30.35 in 1865 to $25.72 in 1866, then declined more slowly until it reached $17.51 in 1876. Thereafter, there was a gradual creep upward to $22.81 in 1885, a level which did not change much during the remainder of the century. The slight improvement during the later years was largely illusory, for business needs expanded more rapidly than did the currency required to supply them, and in the West and South, particularly on the farm, bank credit was not overcoming the deficiency. Largely as a consequence of this situation, the general-price index plummeted from 174 in 1866 to 90 in 1879 (1910-1914 = 100). Then, with various ups and downs, the lowest point of 68 arrived in 1897, after which there was gradual improvement for a few years and then a real upsurge.

All businesses experienced fluctuations between prosperity and depression during these years, but the farmer, more than others, found it difficult to adjust to the changes. He could not lay off the labor force (usually just the family) and abandon half-grown crops because of a market collapse. He could merely redouble his efforts in the hope of breaking even. He had no organization to restrict output and maintain prices, as did the rising industrial monopolies. The nature of the tariff added nothing to his income, but simply raised his living costs. No politicians, even during election campaigns, voted to induce him by liberal subsidies to destroy a crop that would not materialize in any event. Crop insurance had not yet struck the inventive mind.

Even the index of general prices was a delusion. If farm income declined equally with all other earnings, this parity would make even the fixed expenditures more endurable. But at no time between 1860 and 1900 was the farm curve up to the general one. The divergence in 1865 was 37 points. It narrowed somewhat for a few years afterward, but widened again to 30 in 1873. In general-depression periods the gap was not as great as at other times, being only 6 or 8 points during the hard years following the Panic of 1893. The man on the bottom rung of the ladder could not fall as far as the one on the top. At rock bottom, there was no further depth to plumb. But the difference between farm and general-price curves is deceptive. In 1880, for example, agricultural and industrial incomes were each about $5,000,000,000, but farm prices were averaged with the industrial to obtain the general curve. This means that prices of manufactures were as far above the average as farm prices were below it, thus doubling the presumed distance from agricultural parity.

**Grievances Against Railroads and Marketing Agen-**

cies. Another quite pertinent fact is that the prices
quoted on the exchanges were far higher than those paid
to the farmers, particularly in the Midwest, West, and
South. All of the shipping and marketing costs were de-
ducted from the amounts the farmer received. Before
1870 it was calculated that half of each dollar paid for
wheat shipped from west of the Mississippi to the Atlantic
coast went to the middlemen. Transportation charges took
most of the rest. On top of this, the money shortage and
scant credit caused such high interest rates as to make farming hardly attractive. There were times when corn and
wheat growers from Kansas to the Dakotas found it sound
economy to burn the grain to heat their houses. The South
and the trans-Mississippi West endured freight charges
several times as high as those from Chicago eastward. In
1879 the ton-mile rate on the Lake Shore & Michigan
Southern railroad was .64 cents, while on the Burlington
west of Omaha it was six times as much, and on the
Galveston, Houston, and Henderson line it was 4.07 cents.
In 1880 a little railroad in Arkansas and Louisiana
charged 44 cents.

There were other practices of the railroads that made
freight costs to small shippers and to farmers in out-of-
the-way places higher than they might otherwise have
been. Rebates paid to powerful industries not only fostered monopoly growth but had to be paid for by high
rates to the unfavored customers. Most farmers had to
ship from points connected to the market centers by only
one railroad, and often found that they had to pay more
for a short haul than was charged at cities having com-
peting lines for a haul several times as long. Some railroads owned coal mines or other industries, and by trans-
porting their own products without bookkeeping charges,
not only drove their rivals out of business but increased
freight rates for all shippers not in favored groups. Free
passes to politicians, editors, and preachers made for
higher passenger fares for all other riders.

In the early days of the South and West, gullible counties had voted bonds to railroad companies to encourage
building through the locality, and sometimes found themselves obliged to pay off the debt when not a mile of rails
was ever laid. Such practices could do nothing less than
breed discontent. Complaints were also rife about inade-

quate facilities for livestock shipping and against the excessive charges and discriminatory practices of the grain elevators, generally owned by the railroads. The meat packers also received condemnation for fixing prices on livestock. The grain exchanges had clever ways of grading wheat and corn in low classifications when buying and in higher ones when selling, and there were devious ways of rigging the markets that continued throughout the century. The Kansas corn farmer seems to have had some justification for complaining at getting ten cents a bushel for corn that would sell in the East at seventy or eighty. (*See Document No. 14.*)

**Complaints About Credit and Interest Rates.** On top of all this, the credit situation was particularly bad. In the staple-producing sections of the South, the country merchant, who with the passage of time was also usually some large planter, made advances of groceries and supplies to sharecroppers and tenants, and often to neighboring freeholders as well. The ordinary laborer was seldom allowed more than $100 for himself and his family for the year, and this was furnished in supplies charged at approximately double the ordinary retail price asked at independent stores. The contract allowed the merchant a lien on the crop as security and the worker could trade at no other store, since he had no credit at any other and he was perennially short of cash. The landowning farmer got as much credit as it was reasonably certain he would be able to repay, but it was possible to allow just a little more and finally seize the farm for debt. The money was collected from the receipts for the crop when sold by the merchant. This often resulted in small yearly debt balances owed by the more efficient sharecroppers, who then would have to renew the contract in order to keep out of trouble with the law. This made them virtually peons and discouraged them from exerting their best efforts.

But it was not the underdogs at the bottom of the heap who organized for revolt. They were too poor and hopeless to exert the effort. Instead, the small freeholders, faced with the prospect of losing their farms to the store-keepers, after 1880 began joining farmers' alliances that later merged into the Populist movement.

In the newer areas of the Midwest for a score of years after the Civil War, it was not difficult to procure mortgages on farms, but the interest rates were amazingly high. Instead of lowering these charges, the Eastern loan companies hired corps of agents, working on commissions, to induce farmers in the more westerly prairie country, especially north of Indian Territory, to borrow money for expansion purposes. Even after 1900 the rates often ranged between 12% and 15%, while Eastern banks were glad to receive a third or a quarter as much. Yet, as long as land was rising in value and crops were good, farmers swallowed this bait. In the central and western parts of Kansas and Nebraska, and to some extent up into the Dakotas and Minnesota, there was a veritable speculative mania in the early 1880's when prices were improving and the prospects looked bright. Then came a cycle of dry years, beginning in 1886; prices again were on the downgrade; and in the avalanche of mortgage foreclosures even the loan companies could not always recover on their frozen assets.

This situation was not typical of the whole trans-Mississippi West. In most of the area the trouble was in getting intermediate and short loans for the raising and marketing of crops. When obtainable, such loans bore interest rates even higher than those on mortgages. Edwin L. Godkin of *The Nation* and later also of the *New York Evening Post,* with a keen theoretical knowledge of financial matters but no understanding whatever of conditions in the West, as early as 1868 was using his editorial columns to quarrel with the prairie farmers about their complaints. Stop owing money, so went his refrain, and you will not have to worry about credit. The farmers would have been glad to comply, if such action had been as easy as Godkin assumed. Six years later he was even more caustic in denouncing those who asked for enough monetary inflation to ease their financial strain. The government should turn its back firmly and permanently on these greedy seekers for personal gain.

**The Granger Movement.**   Meanwhile farmers' clubs and political parties were springing up in what was then the wheat belt, and especially in Illinois, Wisconsin, Minnesota, and Iowa. In 1867 the clubs in Illinois induced the legislature to enact a law requiring railroads to haul grain from other elevators than their own, thus driving a wedge into one monopoly. Soon, the other states in this group were to join in a series of acts further regulating the railroads. Many of the farmers in these clubs and parties were also members of the Patrons of Husbandry, or Grange, first organized in Washington, D. C., in 1869 by Oliver H. Kelley and some of his fellow government clerks. The Grange was a secret, nonpolitical society, admitting both women and men to the same degrees—the women at a reduced rate, perhaps to assure their joining and not holding the men back from membership. Its purposes were social, educational, and economic, and its aim was to bring some light and cheer into drab lives as well as to work for betterment of living conditions through cooperative enterprises.

The Grange attracted but few members in its early years, but hard times following the Panic of 1873, when farm mortgages were coming due and the usurers would not renew them even at the earlier interest of 15% and 20%, caused farmers to join in droves. They hoped that therein might lie their salvation from bankruptcy and foreclosure. By early 1875 there were 858,000 members, 32 state organizations existed, and there were some members in all of the states except four. The Farmers' Parties, sometimes also called Reform, Independent, or Antimonopoly, began to flourish at this same time. It was easy for grangers to circumvent their society's ban on political activity. All that was necessary was for the members of a local group to organize separately into a branch of the state party, and use the grange hall not only for its stipulated purposes, but as a party rallying place as well. This was called politics "outside the gate," even if it was within the walls.

In some of the states, rival farmers' clubs had greater strength than the Grange, but in the states along the upper Mississippi, the Patrons of Husbandry had the ascendancy, and its members, working through the parties, secured the best-known of the legislation popularly known as the "granger laws." The Warehouse Act of 1867 in Illinois was followed in 1871 by legislation fixing maximum rates for freight and passenger service. When two years later the supreme court of the state invalidated these schedules, the legislature adopted a stricter law so carefully drafted as to escape constitutional objections. Minnesota enacted a similar measure in 1871, and Wisconsin and Iowa did likewise in 1874. The railroads, bitter from the start, carried on a campaign of opposition all the way from the hustings to the highest court in the land. By drastic reduction of services, they made the Wisconsin law so unpopular that it was ultimately repealed. But early in 1877 the United States Supreme Court, in a series of eight decisions on the granger laws, upheld all of the fundamental principles. In *Munn vs. Illinois,* involving the Warehouse Act, the court established the right of a state to regulatory powers. In *Peik vs. Chicago and Northwestern Railroad,* growing out of the Wisconsin law, it went so far as to sanction the fixing of rates by the legislature on interstate shipments originating in the state. In 1886 the court reversed itself on this point, leaving no interstate regulation and thus stimulating the passage of the Interstate Commerce Act by Congress in 1887. This law was too weak to have much effect until reinforced after 1900. But fear of more stringent legislation had some effect, influencing the carriers to correct various rate abuses.

The Grange was not as effective in its cooperative efforts as the Farmers' Parties were in their fight against the railroads. Iowa led the states in the establishment of buying and selling agencies, and the State Grange soon had thirty grain elevators and contracts with factories and wholesalers for reduced prices on mass purchases. In 1872 it established a central agency for such purchases. Illinois grangers by pursuing the same methods were able to buy harvesters for $100 less than the $275 charged by regular merchants. California experimented with cooperative banking. Elsewhere there were efforts at selling fire insurance, while Iowa dabbled in meat packing and flour milling. In the South, there were few attempts of any kind; the country merchants had too tight a grip on credit to tolerate the idea. Then in 1873 the State Grange of Iowa invested in a harvester factory and went on to buy establishments for the making of plows and other implements. In 1874 the members were able to buy about 250 harvesters at half the customary price. By this time, the National Grange was also investing heavily in like ventures.

This movement came to an untimely end in 1875 when the Iowa factories went bankrupt, soon followed by a like fate for the national program. Independent competitors were too powerful for the inexperienced grange managers to cope with; price cutting invited price wars with concerns rich enough to hold out until the cooperatives crumbled; and sales at barely above cost left no reserves for expansion, slack periods, or litigation. Failures of business and manufacturing enterprises caused the owner granges to disband in order to avoid lawsuits over debts, and a general decline in membership set in. Some years later, when the movement began to revive on conservative lines, the greatest membership came in states outside the center of the activities of the 1870's. The Farmers' Parties also fell apart after the success of their legislative program, and in 1876 the bulk of the members were back in the Republican or Democratic fold, determined to save the republic in a more orthodox fashion.

**The Greenback Movement.** Although the greenback movement began in the labor organizations, it had a great appeal and support from farmers in the 1870's. Edward Kellogg had been advocating the idea since 1848, and it entered politics in a tentative manner in 1872 by way of the National Labor Reform Party. It continued with the Greenback and Greenback Labor combinations from 1876 to 1884 and had some feeble support for the next four years. Numerous tinkerings with the currency during the Civil War and afterwards added to the greenback appeal. The $450,000,000 in United States notes (greenbacks) authorized by Congress during the war, and bobbing down and up in volume until 1878, became almost the sole legal tender from 1862 until the country returned to the gold standard in 1879. Some national bank notes appeared after the passage of the National Bank Act of 1863, and two years later the federal tax of 10% on the note issues of the state banks drove most of those institutions into the national system. This did not add to the volume of the currency, but the requirement that national banks must redeem their notes in legal tender on demand gave them a stability in value never possessed by the common run of the state bank notes replaced.

Banks with national charters could deposit federal bonds with the Treasury and receive in exchange notes equal to 90% of the face or market value of the bonds, whichever was the lower. This allowed the banks to collect two interest rates on one investment. The weakness of the system was that it provided a volume of currency that expanded and contracted in reverse order to business needs. In periods of wildcat investment and rising prices, small operators sold their government bonds to the banks, even at a large discount, hoping to get rich in blue-sky ventures. The banks, with this new security, then issued additional notes just at the time when a little deflation was needed to curb speculation. On the other hand, in depression years, persons who had saved something out of the stock-market crashes eagerly bought bonds from the banks, and at a premium, so as to find a safe investment. The banks were glad to oblige by selling at 110 bonds for which they had paid probably 80, but this necessitated a shrinkage of the national currency at a time when expansion was most needed to restore confidence. For many years, this formula worked with almost arithmetical exactness. In the depression following the Panic of 1873, the volume of national bank notes shrank $40,000,000 in two years' time. It rose by $50,000,000 in the more prosperous times of the early 1880's, but slid downward after the depression of the middle of the decade until the shrinkage by 1890 was $190,000,000, and only $162,000,000 was left in circulation.

It was this tendency that made the greenbackers bitter foes of the national banks. These theorists were advocates of a managed currency. They proposed to substitute United States notes for all other money except small change. The greenbacks would be interchangeable at the will of the holder with government bonds paying 3.65% interest (a cent a day on each $100). When general prices showed a downward trend, hard-pressed bondholders would of necessity convert their securities into greenbacks, thus reversing the movement. In good times, more than enough of the little fellows would again buy bonds to offset speculators who were selling them, and again the price curve would level off. Probably because the greenbackers were not as confident of the second part of their hypothesis as they were of the first, they developed a violent hostility to the produce and stock exchanges. The whole idea is an attractive one but for the tendency to overlook the fact, demonstrated so completely in 1933 and following years, that there is always pressure to get the legislators to inflate the currency in periods of depression, but nobody seems to want to apply the brakes when the markets are boom-

ing. However, there is no reason to suppose that the hap-
hazard monetary policies pursued since 1865 have been
any more beneficial than greenbackism would have been.
Certainly, the pure theorists were relatively few in number. The Greenback Party and the voters who supported
it were rank opportunists, rarely considering the long-
range view.

Evidence of farmer support of the theory comes with
the "Ohio Idea" of 1868. Representative Samuel F. Carey
of Ohio developed the issue that carried the name of
George H. Pendleton of the same state, that the Treasury
of the United States should pay off the principal of the
government bonds, as they fell due, in greenbacks instead
of gold. The wartime contract profiteers had bought the
bonds with greenbacks worth 40 cents to the dollar in gold,
had received interest in gold (thus converting the presumed 6% into an actual 15%) and now expected a
capital bonus of from 100% to 150% by cashing the
bonds in gold. At the same time, the farmer selling his hay
at Fort Riley, for example, was getting depreciated greenbacks in payment. The slogan of the backers of the Ohio
Idea was "the same currency for the bondholder as for
the plowholder." They did not achieve their goal, but the
support given by western farmers to the idea helped cut
Ulysses S. Grant's popular vote for the Presidency far
below the ratio of his electoral majority.

Further discontent grew out of the Resumption Act of
1875, one feature of which was to reduce the volume of
greenbacks from the existing $382,000,000 to $300,000,-
000. In a clumsy effort to disguise this deflation, $5 in
national bank notes was to replace each $4 in greenback
retirement. This subterfuge did not fool the debtors of the
West and South. They realized that it would only cushion
the deflationary tendency. As the public debt was paid off,
the national bank notes would be retired and $82,000,000
in greenbacks would be replaced by nothing. So strong
did the protest become that by an Act of May 31, 1878,
Congress repealed this cremation feature of the Resumption Act, leaving $346,681,016 greenback dollars in circu-
lation—a figure that, on the books, remained perpetual
thereafter. The further history of the Resumption Act and
the resumption of specie payments in 1879 is not important for these pages.

The greenback issue in national politics became a fiasco in 1872 when David Davis of Illinois withdrew from the nomination for the Presidency by the National Labor Reform Party, which then collapsed. In 1876 the Greenback Party nominated the 85-year-old capitalist and philanthropist Peter Cooper of New York and, as his running mate, Samuel F. Carey. But this was a poor year for third-party candidates. Farmers and laborers could postpone their utopian dreams for a while and stick to their accustomed Democratic or Republican connections for a while, so as to save the republic in the great Hayes-Tilden election. Also, Cooper disappointed them by failing to provide his own campaign fund. He got only 82,000 votes. The most promising year was 1878, when the Presidency was not at stake and when the inflationists were feeling profound disgust for the failure of their dream as it took shape in the Bland-Allison Silver Purchase Act. They polled over a million votes, and by coalition mainly with Democrats, elected fourteen Representatives to Congress. Iowa alone gave them 124,000 votes, and though the next three high counts were in Massachusetts, Pennsylvania, and New York, in proportion to the total electorate in the different states the ratio was highest in the agricultural West.

In 1880 the Democrats were seeking revenge for the "stolen election" of 1876-1877, and the Republicans were again waving the bloody shirt to save the republic from the forces of rebellion. In James B. Weaver of Iowa the Greenbackers had an abler candidate than either of the greater rivals, but once again the farmers felt obliged to return to their old allegiances in a crisis. Weaver got less than 308,000 votes and the Greenback delegation in Congress dropped to ten. Two years later there were only four Independents and one Greenbacker, and in 1884, two Independents of Greenback leanings. In that year Benjamin F. Butler was the candidate, and his career, political and otherwise, for the preceding quarter of a century had not been such as to inspire unshakable confidence. He emerged with 134,000 votes—18,000 less than went to the Prohibitionist candidate John P. St. John of Kansas. In 1888 the rag, tag, and bobtail of the party assembled again in convention, restated their principles, and then closed shop several years after the customers had deserted to the free-silver movement.

**Early Phases of the Free-Silver Movement.** Ever since the Coinage Act of 1834 had undervalued silver, the amount of that metal in a dollar had been worth more than the coin itself. Owners of bullion sold it for industrial uses rather than take it to the mint, and owners of dollars were prone to melt them down for the same market. The surplus value had ranged between 5.22 and 1.83 cents, and stood at 2.25 just before February 12, 1873, when Congress put a stop to the coining of any silver dollars except a limited number of extra-heavy ones for settling trade balances with Oriental countries that were on the silver standard. Even this practice ended a few years later, when the reduced value of the metal made the new coins attractive for domestic use. Demonetization occurred, purposefully, just at a time when Western mines were beginning to pour huge quantities of silver on the market and when several European states were going either partially or wholly on the single gold standard. The financial interests responsible for the Act of 1873 had the world situation well in mind, but the ordinary citizen, who seldom saw a silver dollar, let the event pass without notice. President Grant forgot he had signed such a measure, and later in the year, when the trade balances were adverse after the Panic and money was flowing outward to Europe, expressed wonder that the mine owners were not pouring bullion into the mints. (*See Document No. 15.*)

By that time, the commercial value of silver had dropped below par with the dollar, and owners of the metal would have been glad to take the extra value at the mints. As the price continued to fall, a cry arose about the "Crime of '73," and continued to echo for a quarter of a century. Indebted farmers were quick to pick up the chorus of the mine owners. They continued to note also, that, as silver continued to decline in value, farm prices kept even pace. Obviously, it was gold, and not silver, that was out of pace with the general economy. Gold-standard advocates argued that a return to the free and unlimited coinage of silver, such as had always prevailed before 1873, would flood the United States with the silver of

the world and cause unlimited inflation. Yet even when
the gold value of the silver dollar fell to 49 cents in the
late 1890's, it was still adhering closely to the curve of
general prices. This would indicate that free coinage
would have maintained a horizontal general-price level
instead of a downward slope. But the additional market
for silver in the coinage would have narrowed the ratio
with gold, making both metals necessary to sustain business needs. Most of the horror conjured up by the financiers about free silver was simple hysteria.

The greenback idea, sanely applied, would have been a
surer guarantee of stability, but free silver had a stronger
appeal to people of untutored minds. It would be a return
to the standard of their fathers and, anyway, the ring of
the precious metals in the pocket was more reassuring
than the rustling of seemingly worthless paper. Representative Richard P. ("Silver Dick") Bland of Missouri,
having worked as a youth in the western mines, assumed
the leadership in Congress for the prompt repeal of the
Act of 1873. He had support from well-known men of both
major parties. Among the Republicans, there were William
D. ("Pig Iron") Kelley of Pennsylvania, Jay A. ("My
Dear") Hubbell, the later Speaker of the House Joseph
Warren Keifer of Ohio, and William McKinley, also from
Ohio and later to be shanghaied into the gold-standard
ranks. In fact, Kelley worked hand in hand with Bland in
1876-1878 for free and unlimited coinage of silver at the
ratio of 16 to 1 with gold. Among the Democratic supporters of the bill were John G. Carlisle of Kentucky (also
later to be Speaker), Jacob D. Cox of Ohio, Samuel S.
("Sunset") Cox of New York, and Simon Bolivar Buckner
of Kentucky, later, like McKinley, to switch over to gold.

In the Senate, Bland's bill got a working over by a
committee headed by William B. Allison of Iowa, and the
Bland-Allison Act, passed on February 28, 1878, over the
veto of President Rutherford B. Hayes, was a sore disappointment to the free-silver men. But they thought it a
little better than no concession at all. The measure ordered
the Secretary of the Treasury to buy silver at the rate of
from $2,000,000 to $4,000,000 worth each month and
have it coined immediately into dollars interchangeable
with silver certificates. The difference between the cost of
the bullion and the value of the dollars was profit to the

Treasury instead of to the mine operators as had been the case before 1873. Each President (Hayes, Garfield, Arthur, Cleveland, and Harrison) until a change in the law in 1890 was a gold-standard man, sponsoring the purchase of only the prescribed minimum. One feature of the law gave some comfort to the silver men. The lower the price of silver fell, the more $2,000,000 would buy and the more dollars would go into circulation, the inflationary effect of which would tend to check further decline in all prices, including that of silver. But, quite naturally, they preferred purchases at the allowable maximum. Even at the minimum, as the silver market declined, the coinage each month in 1889 was half a million dollars more than that in 1880. (*See Document No. 15.*)

**The Rise of the Farmers' Alliances.** Before there was any more legislative juggling of silver, the farmers of the West and South were organized as never before. The first steps of any significance were in 1880, when Milton George, publisher of the *Western Rural* at Chicago, sponsored the founding of the National Farmers' Alliance, generally called the Northwestern Alliance, and an earlier movement got a new start in Texas and went through a succession of names culminating with the National Farmers' Alliance and Industrial Union, but popularly known as the Southern Alliance. Both of these movements began with the farmers themselves and grew and broadened their scope under the same impulse. Milton George, as the guiding spirit of the Northwestern group, borrowed from the social and educational features of the Grange, but eschewing its secrecy and avoidance of direct political action, stressed the economic and political approach. Within a year the Northwestern Alliance claimed a thousand local groups containing 24,500 members, largely centered in the North Central states. In another few months, the lodges doubled in number and quadrupled in membership. There was a Negro branch in Arkansas, organized on race lines not by George's preference but because in the South he could succeed in no other way.

A drouth in Iowa, Nebraska, and Kansas led to rapid growth there in 1881 and 1882. Then, for a year or two, interest declined, only to be followed by remarkable expansion resulting from low prices in the wheat belt in the later 1880's. By 1890 there were 130,000 members in

Kansas, while the Dakotas and Minnesota were not far behind. Since 1887 the Alliance had been talking free silver and federal competition in the railroad business. Dalliance with the Knights of Labor brought no union. Thereafter Milton George was no longer the leader, but he continued to oppose union with the Southern Alliance, particularly resenting its success in its inroads on the membership in Kansas and the Dakotas. Growing up alongside the Northwestern Alliance was the Farmers' Mutual Benefit Association, which started out from southern Illinois in 1883 and was most active east of the Mississippi River, concentrating on cooperative selling and boasting a membership of half a million after 1890. There was also a Patrons of Industry, still farther to the east, that did not figure largely in the general movement except that it had a number of successful cooperatives.

The behemoth of them all was the Southern Alliance. Beginning in 1878 as a union of small cooperatives into the Grand State Alliance of Texas, it soon fell apart over differences of opinion about endorsing greenbackism. In 1880 with a new charter as a secret and benevolent society, it had a rapid growth, reaching 1200 lodges with 50,000 members in the next five years. From early days it opposed the crop-lien system of the country stores, as a means of realizing larger returns from crops. In 1886 when C. W. Macune joined, it was already beginning a campaign for increased taxes on land speculators, including the railroads, the extermination of land monopolies under foreign control, more paper money, the abolition of dealing in futures, and other planks to go into the later Populist platform. By 1887 Macune was in control and set about merging with the Louisiana Farmers' Union. In 1888 came the absorption of the Agricultural Wheel, which in the preceding five or six years had expanded from a little debating society in Arkansas into a presumed membership of 500,000 in eight states. It contributed proposals for crop limitation at a time when later advocates, Herbert C. Hoover and Franklin D. Roosevelt, were little boys. It was hostile to tariff protection, national banks, and corporations, and urged the readoption of a graduated income tax, thus sawing further Populist planks.

In 1889 the new combination assumed its permanent name, and in 1890 it proclaimed a membership of 3,000,-

000, in addition to the independent Farmers' Clubs sponsored by Benjamin R. ("Pitchfork Ben") Tillman in South Carolina, with which it collaborated. But it would have no direct connection with the Colored Farmers' National Alliance and Cooperative Union, a combination of Negro groups effected at Houston in 1886. Four years later, this organization claimed 1,250,000 members. It, and the Southern Alliance as well, must have been enrolling entire families, for in some areas there were fewer farms than alleged alliance members. Certainly no great proportion were voters, for rarely before 1890 were they able to swing elections. Race lines came before class solidarity, and as usual, the zeal for maintaining white supremacy worked against the hope of attaining economic improvement for all or any.

Macune was in control of the Southern Alliance less than three years, but in that time his experiments with cooperative marketing led him to evolve the subtreasury plan for which he is best known. The Texas Alliance from its earliest days had developed upon the still earlier granger plans of escaping from reliance on the country merchants in the selling of cotton. First, alliance business agents tried county-wide agreements with selected dealers; then they attempted to handle sales themselves. This led to a state exchange for the coordination of efforts. Continued low prices after 1885 inspired additional business activities. But a fifth of the sales revenue still went to middlemen and another fifth by way of fraudulent weighing, low-grading, confiscatory transportation charges, and the like. Then, the Alliance tried direct sales at county cotton yards, direct to Eastern purchasers, the yards soon coming under State Alliance supervision. By 1887 Macune realized that the success of this plan was limited by the lack of sufficient capital to give buyers the assurance that the farmers could live up to their contracts. For the next two years Macune tried to build up a Farmers' Alliance Exchange with $500,000 capital, but the inability of the members to raise more than 3.4% of this amount led to the failure of the Exchange in 1890.

Macune surrendered control of the Alliance in 1889, to edit its national newspaper, *The Economist,* at Washington. There he worked out the details of the subtreasury scheme, evolving it out of a less ambitious plan he had not had time to apply in Texas and which the Alliance had not been wealthy enough to finance. He would have the federal government establish a subtreasury, warehouse, and elevator in each county of the nation that produced each year $500,000 worth of grain, cotton, tobacco, wool, or sugar, or any combination of these crops. Instead of the United States Treasury depositing surplus funds in the national banks, it should employ these subtreasuries, where farmers could deposit warehouse receipts for the enumerated nonperishable products and receive in exchange loans, at 1% interest, in treasury notes specially provided for the purpose, equaling 80% of the current market value of the goods. The loans would expire in not more than a year, by which time the stored crops must be sold and the notes retired.

The buyer would pay the farmer the difference between the purchase price and the advance made on the warehouse receipts, as well as the balance owed at the subtreasury for the loan, including the interest and storage and insurance charges, thus wiping out the obligations to the government. In the meantime, the notes would pass as legal tender, thus giving the farmer the funds for the growing of another crop while waiting for the market to reach its peak, instead of dumping his year's produce on the market during the glutted harvest season. This would relieve Northern farmers of reliance on uncertain bank credit and Southerners of dependence on the country merchants. The notes, when redeemed, would be reissued against the next year's crop, and thus would not become a spiraling medium of inflation. This plan was not widely different from that of the United States Warehouse Act of August, 1916, greatly extended after 1933, but in 1890 it was considered radical. (*See Document No. 16.*)

Armed with this proposal, Macune attended the convention of the Southern Alliance held at St. Louis in December, 1889. At the same time and in the same city, representatives of the Northwestern Alliance, the Colored Alliance, the Farmers' Mutual Benefit Association, and the Knights of Labor also convened to try to work out some sort of merger. The American Federation of Labor would take no part at all in an assemblage that encompassed employing farmers, and the Knights of Labor would go no further than an expression of solidarity. The Colored

Alliance could make no headway with the Southern Alliance. The Northwestern Alliance feared submergence if joined with the huge Southern organization, and besides did not approve of the latter's secrecy and race exclusiveness. Furthermore, Macune could not interest the Northern group in his subtreasury plan. On the other hand, the Southern men were interested in cottonseed oil and could not approve the Northern proposal to ban its use in substitutes for lard and butter. Things that both alliances could agree to included a managed greenback currency, free silver, abandonment of the national banks, government ownership of the railroad and telegraph lines, the recapture of railroad land grants, the abolition of alien landowning and of market dealings in grain futures, and government economies that would remove the props from under the protective tariff. There was more or less of agreement on a graduated income tax and on labor reforms, but the Southern Alliance alone accepted the subtreasury idea.

**The Sherman Silver-Purchase Act of 1890.** There was no agreement at St. Louis on concerted political activity, but farmers' parties in several states began making preparations for the campaign of 1890. For a time, the two greater rivals went their separate ways, while the Kansas and Dakota state organizations switched wholly to the Southern Alliance. The Populist Party was soon to absorb them both, anyway. In the meanwhile, their influence, strengthened by a dozen new free-silver senators, was enough to sway Congress to the passage of the Sherman Silver-Purchase Act. Late in 1889 and early in 1890, Congress admitted Washington, Montana, the two Dakotas, Idaho, and Wyoming to the union, and their unanimous block of votes made a free-silver body of the Senate, which in 1878 had mutilated the Bland measure. John Sherman had almost nothing to do with the shaping or passage of the law to which the public attached his name (as, with like disregard for realities, they did to the antitrust measure of the same year). The new act, approved on July 14, 1890, was presumably only an amendment to the Bland-Allison Act, but the changes were so significant as to constitute an entirely different approach.

The monthly purchases now were to be 4,500,000 ounces of silver. Unlike the earlier plan, the volume would remain constant whether the price rose or fell. Still more important was the fact that the bullion would be bought with new treasury notes, redeemable in silver or gold, and none of the silver was to be coined unless to replace and retire those notes as conversion was demanded. Any persons asking gold would get it, but in that case the treasury notes would remain in circulation. But, ironically and inconsistently enough, the mine owners demanded gold, and got it. Consequently almost no silver was coined, and it did not add to the monetary supply. Only the cost was of inflationary effect, and the lower silver fell in value the smaller was the inflation. This was exactly the reverse of the manner of operation of the Bland-Allison Act. Until the repeal of purchases three years later, the bullion simply piled up in the treasury vaults, creating an embarrassing problem about ultimate disposal. (*See Document No. 15.*)

The free-silver men realized the weaknesses of the law, but since they could not get what they wanted in the House of Representatives, they accepted it because at the then prevailing price of silver, it would put more money in circulation than would the minimum purchases under the Bland-Allison Act. In their own interest they would have done better to insist on an amendment, one sentence in length, repealing the minimum and retaining the maximum of the old law as mandatory. With this change, the monthly addition to the stock of money in 1890 would have been $4,944,376 instead of the $4,738,500 provided by the Sherman Act. As silver continued to decline in succeeding months and years, the mistake became more glaringly obvious. At the price in 1894, even the minimum purchases under the Bland-Allison principle would have added $4,073,319 to the monetary supply monthly, while the Sherman Act would have contributed only $2,880,000, had either measure still been in force. By that time, it was evident that it would have been better for the silver men in 1890 to have blocked any change in the law of 1878, as they could have easily done when they failed to get their full demand.

**The Populist Movement.**  Nothing daunted by disappointment with the silver debacle, the Alliance men and their allies plunged into the political campaign of 1890, determined on correcting the situation. The farmers' party of Kansas called itself People's, that of South Dakota was Independent, and the one in Nebraska chose the name People's Independent. Elsewhere in the West, the name of Industrial Party was heard. Ben Tillman, with his verbal pitchfork, was prodding the farmers' clubs of South Carolina to a fury, and Georgia was up in arms for full revolt. Kansas, in its usually predictable fashion, had a veritable circus for itself. The not always demure Mary E. Lease went about the state pounding home the sound economic doctrine that the farmers should "raise less corn and more HELL." The clerical-looking and ordinarily immaculately dressed Jerry Simpson, making capital of the charge that he was "Sockless," donned scarecrow raiment and defeated his "silk-stockinged" rival and sartorial critic James R. Hallowell in a race for Congress. William A. Peffer, whose whiskers were so luxuriant that none could tell whether he wore a shirt, ousted the veteran John J. Ingalls who had served three full terms in the Senate. In fact, the Jayhawkers took Mrs. Lease's admonition so literally as to cause the prim E. L. Godkin to express the pious hope that Congress would admit no more states to the union until Kansas became civilized.

The Independents, gaining control of the legislature of South Dakota, sent the preacher James H. Kyle to the Senate to join "Whiskers" Peffer of Kansas and John L. M. Irby of South Carolina. The Southern Alliance fought shy of third-party movements, fearing a division in the forces upholding white supremacy, and preferred trying to capture the Democratic organizations. This they succeeded in doing rather effectively in most of the states, sending 35 or more Democrats to the House of Representatives pledged to Alliance policies and to join the eight farmers' party representatives from the West. The 52 representatives claimed for the two sections combined, included some elected by fusion of parties. Additional gains were the three senators already named, three governors, both houses of seven state legislatures and the lower house in half a dozen more. Elated by this promise of early victory, there was soon a widespread effort at the creation of a national political party. At a convention at Ocala, Florida, in December, 1890, the dominant Southern Alliance rejected suggestions of the delegates from the Knights of Labor for such a party, but made some

concessions toward cooperation with the F.M.B.A. and
the Colored Alliance, though there was nothing like a
merger. The resolutions adopted were quite similar to
those of the St. Louis Convention of a year earlier. (*See
Documents Nos. 17 and 18.*)

Despite the coolness shown at Ocala toward political
action, some 1400 delegates from 32 states met at Cincinnati on May 19, 1891, and supported the call of an
early Omaha convention that resulted in the Washington's
Birthday convention at St. Louis in 1892, for the formation of the People's Party (Populist). At Omaha on July
4, following, the Populists nominated Weaver of Iowa and
James G. Field of Virginia to head their national ticket,
and adopted a platform incorporating nearly all of the
Alliance demands of previous years. It was short and
unequivocal, demanding the subtreasury system or something better, greenbacks to replace national bank notes,
free silver, a circulating medium of not less than $50
per capita, a postal-savings system, rigid economy in
government, a constitutional amendment to establish a
universal civil-service system, and the recovery of all
land held by any corporations beyond their actual needs
and all land owned by aliens. Further resolutions called
for improved legislation against contract labor, the exclusion of undesirable immigrants, a shorter working day
for industrial laborers, the abolition of the Pinkerton
system of labor spies, the endorsement of the Knights of
Labor label, the adoption of the initiative and referendum,
and a single term for the President and Vice-President.
Previous conventions had already recommended the direct
election of senators, but had displayed only flirtatious
interest in woman suffrage. (*See Document No. 19.*)

The appeal to labor captured not many ballots except
in the Northwest, though Weaver got some votes in every
one of the states except Delaware. Out of the total of
1,027,000 (9% of the vote for all parties) Kansas contributed 163,000, Texas nearly 100,000, Alabama 85,000,
Nebraska 83,000, Colorado almost 54,000, and North
Carolina about 45,000, these six accounting for more than
half. Georgia, Missouri, and Minnesota brought it to
two thirds, and the addition of Oregon, South Carolina,
Tennessee, and Kentucky made one third of the states
casting three quarters of the vote. Counting Missouri as

Southern, as was often done in those days, half of the fourteen leaders were in the South, and four tenths of the Populist presidential vote came from that section. But all of the 22 electoral votes for Weaver and Field came from the West. The Democrats did not have a national ticket in Colorado, Idaho, Kansas, North Dakota, or Wyoming, and Weaver carried the first three of these as well as Nevada and one elector each from North Dakota and Oregon. He lost Nebraska by less than a hundred votes.

In spite of the aggregate large showing in the South, no state delivered more than 37% of its vote to the Populist national candidates. The erratic Tillman and his followers, with all their hatred of the gold-standard Grover Cleveland, gave him South Carolina's electors in order to save white supremacy, and the Populists got only 2400 ballots. On the other hand, the later Negro hater Thomas E. Watson of Georgia fairly groveled before the black man to gain his support, but here the Democrats beat Watson at his own game. They saved both Alabama and Georgia by marching huge controlled blocks of Negroes to the polls to maintain the *status quo* in race relations. For a brief time, the black man seemed in a grotesque way actually to be attaining the promise of the Fifteenth Amendment. But the horrified afterthoughts of the Bourbon Democrats soon wrought a reversal in this trend. The way to maintain white supremacy and to avert further Populist revolt was to use subterfuges to disfranchise all poor men, whether black or white. On the national scene the Populists elected five senators and ten representatives to Congress, who were reinforced by some Southern Democrats supported by the Alliance. To these may be added the governors Davis R. Waite of Colorado, Lorenzo D. Lewelling of Kansas, and Eli Shortridge of North Dakota, along with the Democratic but like-minded Tillman of South Carolina. In all, about 50 state officials and 1500 state legislators and county officials added to the toll.

It would be more entertaining than edifying to recall the stories of Lewelling's battle over the control of the Kansas legislature, the discharge of the entire faculty of the Kansas State Agricultural College and the rehiring of only such ones as were not obnoxious to the Populists, and the contest in Colorado that won for Waite the sobriquet of "Bloody Bridles." More important is the fact that in 1892 the Populists were as near to success as they were ever destined to come as a party. They increased their vote by nearly a half in 1894 and elected seven representatives and six senators to Congress, in addition to a few sympathetic Southern Democrats, such as Tillman, who went to the Senate threatening to stick his pitchfork in Cleveland's ribs. But compared with 1890 and 1892, this was no real gain. Their enemies were combining forces against them, and any move to control any activity above the local level was getting increasingly more hopeless. It may be that in 1896 they scared the Democrats into an endorsement of free silver and the income tax, but it is more realistic to aver that the Populists sold their souls and their more important platform planks for this mess of pottage.

In an account of farmers' movements, the election of 1896 is hardly worth a mention. As Senator Marion Butler of North Carolina warned the Populist convention, the surrender of party identity would soon result in Democratic repudiation of any Populist taint. Even if William Jennings Bryan had won, free silver was only a lesser demand of the farmers, and there is no reason to suppose they would have gained anything else. But the partial fusion with the Democrats in 1896 ruined the Populists' effectiveness. Tom Watson struggled along with a remnant of the once great following until 1908, by which time even he had to admit defeat. In national legislation the Populists had gained exactly nothing. The graduated income tax, forced down Democratic throats in 1894, was the nearest approach, but the Supreme Court threw it out a year later. On the other hand, the prophetic insight of the Populist leaders is seen in the piecemeal adoption of the bulk of their platform by perfectly respectable Congresses in the early decades of the twentieth century. Even inflation, beyond the wildest hopes of the Populists, came, but not by the way of free silver, which itself must inevitably have come about sooner or later had not a multiplication of the world's gold output, a modification of the greenback idea, and the essence of the subtreasury system made it superfluous.

**The End of the Silver Controversy.** In the meantime, Congress held a firm line on the single gold standard, and wavered slightly only once on the matter of silver coinage. Following the Panic of 1893, Cleveland found that the drains on the gold reserve for settling foreign-trade balances were reaching threatening proportions. On several occasions he sold bonds to procure gold to bolster the reserve, though he could see no merit whatever in the Populist Jacob S. Coxey's argument that the government should follow a like policy for public works to provide employment for America's hungry millions of idle men and their families. Instead, when Coxey's depleted army reached Washington in 1894, he and some of his lieutenants were arrested for stepping on the grass of the Capitol lawn, where millions had trod unmolested. In order to prevent the operators of silver mines from continuing their raids on the gold reserve through conversion of treasury notes, in 1893 Cleveland induced Congress to repeal the purchase clause of the Sherman Act of 1890.

For five years thereafter the bullion in the treasury vaults remained an embarrassing problem. Then in 1898 the Senate, still having a free-silver majority, forced the inclusion of a rider on a military-appropriation act. This ordered the coinage of at least 1,500,000 silver dollars monthly until the supply vanished. This point arrived twelve years later. As dollars were minted, they replaced treasury notes, but that left a surplus of silver representing the difference between its cost as bullion at purchase and its coin value. Thus in the long run a part of the Bland-Allison principle triumphed. Even with this added increment, all the silver bought after 1878 really added little to the money supply. The increase in gold and certificates in circulation to 1900 was a third more than that of silver and its certificates and treasury notes combined. In 1900 Congress passed the Gold Standard Act which put the country on a single metallic basis by which all other money was measured until 1933, when the gold standard passed away perhaps forever, except as a tenuous theory.

# MOVEMENTS SINCE 1900

**Beginnings of the Farmers' Union.** With the passing of the Alliances and the collapse of the Populist movement, there was some salvage from the earnest evangelism of the late departed in the rise of new organizations, at first less opportunistic, and bent on maintaining economic parity for farmers. Chief of these were the Farmers' Educational and Cooperative Union and the American Society of Equity, both founded in 1902. By this date the hard times of the dismal nineties were in the background. Agriculture, in general, was entering a period of well-being such as the oldest farmers could not remember. There was general improvement until 1914, and then, influenced by war and world chaos, came a mighty upsurge that ended in disaster by 1921. But even in the lush years, all was not well. There were localized sore spots and a general feeling that the spread in prices between the producers and the consumers of farm goods was too great. Hence, the central effort of the first decade and a half of the century was on cooperative enterprise, particularly in marketing.

The Farmers' Union was founded in Rains County, Texas, by Isaac Newton Gresham, a former organizer for the Farmers' Alliance, and ten associates. It received a state charter on August 28, 1902. The purpose was to control marketing so as to get better prices. It cost a dollar to join, and monthly dues were five cents, but for the first few years the small cost of membership did not enable the organization to spread outside the Southern states. With the death of Gresham in 1906, Charles S. Barrett of Georgia came into control and, the Texas domination permanently broken, activities began to expand. Soon the Union had business agents, cooperative stores, cotton warehouses, grain elevators, and flour mills. Better prices were expected to come from withholding sales when markets were sluggish. Campaigns for cotton-acreage reduction were combined with attempts to sell directly to American and foreign factories. In England the Union had offices at Liverpool and Manchester. Expanded business ventures included the purchase of a coal mine and the establishment of a Farmers' Bank and Trust Company. Some of these efforts were not particularly successful, and in 1919 the board of directors advised concentration on state and regional produce exchanges, wholesale business houses, cooperative stores, and livestock and grain commissions.

The difficulties of the Farmers' Union in the organization of cooperatives among unprogressive Southern cotton growers made expansion into the North Central states not only desirable but almost imperative if highly successful businesses were to evolve as an exemplary incentive to the more backward areas. The first successful invasions were into Missouri, Illinois, and Kansas, after which, in 1910, there was an unsuccessful attempt to merge with the American Society of Equity. The next movement was into Nebraska and Iowa, the Cornhusker branch at least initially becoming one of the most conservative. Thereafter, entry into the Dakotas, Minnesota, and Wisconsin was not difficult. The Union limited political activity to agitation and lobbying in the state and national capitals for government loans direct to farmers without the use of middlemen, a more equitable distribution of income, limitations on land monopolies, government ownership or control of all mineral resources, and government ownership and operation of the railroads. Further notice of the Farmers' Union will follow a consideration of some other parallel movements.

**The American Society of Equity and Its Offshoots.** While the Farmers' Union was taking root in the South, the American Society of Equity was sprouting in the Midwest. James A. Everitt, a feed and seed merchant of Indianapolis and publisher of *Up-to-Date Farming and Gardening,* was the founder, and the date was December 24, 1902. Everitt's plan was for orderly marketing throughout the year, to replace disastrous crop dumping immediately after harvest. His journal would publish crop reports, gathered from the local Equity units, to serve as marketing guides. Growth of the movement was much slower than Everitt anticipated, and at its peak the membership has been variously estimated at anything from 30,000 to 100,000. By 1908 there were branches in most of the North Central states. But before this, the organization had revolted against what it called dictatorial leadership and misapplication of funds, and in 1907 C. M. Barnett of Kentucky became head. Then Everitt started the rival Farmers' Society of Equity. Thereafter, both groups suffered from competition until the seceders ceased to function in 1916. Under Barnett the American Society decentralized into state units, stressing cooperative marketing and buying. Another schism came in Illinois in 1910 when C. O. Drayton founded the Farmers' Equity Union, which centered its attention on local equity exchanges and had a long, if undistinguished, career. There was also the Equity Cooperative Exchange, an agency of the original American Society of Equity, later to be associated with the Nonpartisan League in North Dakota.

The main cooperative projects of the parent body were grain marketing and livestock shipping, but it also operated elevators, warehouses, meat-packing plants, flour mills, creameries, cheese factories, wool pools, beef rings, buying clubs, cooperative stores, and other enterprises, including insurance companies. Participation in politics was limited to resolutions, petitions, lobbying in the legislative bodies on a strictly opportunistic basis, and questioning and endorsing or disapproving candidates. Until coalescence with the Farmer's Union in 1934 it remained essentially a Midwestern organization, its main strength being in Wisconsin, Minnesota, the Dakotas, Montana, and northern Iowa. In its later stages it was confined largely to Wisconsin, where it joined in the La Follette movement. After 1907 the influence of the national body was never very important, each state group going largely its own way.

**The Kentucky Night Riders.** This extreme decentralization left the Kentucky Equity to indulge in some violent activity, in its opposition to the price-fixing policy of the American Tobacco Company, that brought the Equity into disrepute. Since 1904 there had been a Dark Tobacco District Planters' Protective Association in Kentucky and Tennessee. It included both large and small producers, owners and tenants, blacks and whites. Their one rule, in the effort to combat the trust, was that members must deliver their tobacco to the association's pool and, if necessary, restrict production. Besides farmers, they signed up local officials, professional men, and others not engaged in tobacco growing but more or less personally interested in its prosperity. The tobacco companies rewarded small growers in the hill country by allowing them better prices if they failed to join. These the association members referred to as "Hill Billies."

In 1906 the Kentucky Equity endorsed the attack on the monopoly and strove for control of the local associations. In October of that year a small group of farmers established the Possum Hunters' Organization, which soon changed its name to Night Riders, their purpose being to compel the Hill Billies to conform to the restriction campaign. In 1907 the Night Riders, by agitation and violence, helped the Equity-sponsored Burley Tobacco Society to secure 58% of the crop. The society then determined to grow no tobacco at all in 1908, and utilized the Night Riders to give effect to the decree. Following the pattern of the plant cutters of more than two centuries earlier, they also used whips and sometimes rifles on the recalcitrants, beat up purchasing agents of the trust, fired factories, dynamited machinery, and destroyed hotbeds. Some deaths resulted, but the prosecutors found it impossible to fix responsibility. The outcome was that in November of 1908 the American Tobacco Company and the Burley Tobacco Society came to terms satisfactory to the producers. Between 60,000,000 and 70,000,000 pounds of the weed changed hands for a price of above $12,000,000. In 1909 court action, state militia, volunteer defense guards, and public disapproval checked further activity. Internal dissension followed in the Burley Tobacco Society, which disrupted in consequence. This also brought the end of the Equity in Kentucky. (*See Document No. 20.*)

**The Nonpartisan League.** In the next decade the Equity Cooperative Exchange, failing to get the legislature of North Dakota to establish a state-owned terminal elevator, provided the inspiration that led to the rise of the Farmers' Nonpartisan Political League, generally shortened to Nonpartisan League. North Dakota, famous for its spring wheat since the late 1870's, was pretty well crowded out of the generally fair condition in which American farmers found themselves in the second decade of the century. It was an almost purely agricultural state, but farmers had little to say about how it was run. A little group of grain dealers, millers, and railroad operators of Minneapolis and St. Paul, centered in the Minneapolis Chamber of Commerce and seconded by the Duluth Board of Trade, cracked the whip that made the North Dakota legislatures jump. From early days of statehood and down to 1906, Alexander McKenzie of North Dakota had been the straw boss who passed commands to the local solons, and for another decade the McKenzie ring held its grip.

This clique effectively stifled all attempts at state legislation that might give the wheat growers any chance to cope with the terminal dealers in the Twin Cities and Duluth. These dealers and their agents controlled nearly all the elevators, fixed prices, stifled cooperatives and all independent marketing efforts, and pursued other deleterious practices. These included bogus middlemen to multiply commissions on each bushel of grain, rigged markets, fictitious charges for the switching of cars, grading wheat low on purchase and high on resale, excessive weight deductions for impurities, and using false weights and more ingenious methods of stealing. In 1916 President John H. Worst of the North Dakota Agricultural College declared that this system was costing a state of 600,000 people $55,000,000 a year, or approximately $500 a family, and more than this for each farm family. At the same time, freight rates were nearly twice as high in North Dakota as in Iowa and far above those in Minnesota, South Dakota, and Nebraska. Boxcars provided for shipping grain were often leaky, and payments for the shipments were based on weight at arrival. Interest paid to banks by farmers were often fantastically above the legal maximum of 6%, sometimes up to 25% or 50%, while commercial loans rarely exceeded the legal rate. By state law, usury was not a crime, but the overcharged farmer could sue for recovery of the excess, and in consequence suffer blacklisting on any future loans. (*See Document No. 21.*)

In spite of the opposition of the dealers' ring, between

1910 and 1912 the farmers felt that they had made inroads against their worst enemy by obtaining an amendment to the state constitution permitting the state to build, own, and operate terminal elevators in Minnesota, Wisconsin, or both. With such facilities at Minneapolis, Milwaukee, Duluth, or Superior, other evils of the grain trade could easily be corrected by further state legislation. But the state assembly delayed action that would put the mandate into effect, and in 1915 it was in session considering a huge adverse report on the entire project. The state branch of the American Society of Equity was in session at Bismarck at the same time, determined to exert pressure. But George S. Loftus of the Equity Cooperative Exchange so irked the solons by the pugnacity of his approach that they defeated the elevator bill. At this time, somebody spread the erroneous report that one of the legislators, named Treadwell Twichell, had advised the farmers to "go home and slop the hogs." This admonition, attached to so quaint a name, became the slogan and rallying cry of the Nonpartisan League during its ensuing years of success.

A. E. Bowen, who had once been the Socialist candidate for governor, had long been talking with fellow members of the Equity about getting control of the state government by working within the old parties. Thus he developed the rudiments of the Nonpartisan League. But it was Arthur C. Townley, also an Equity man, a Socialist party organizer, and a friend and associate of Bowen, who had the energy and genius to develop the idea, create the League, and push it to temporary ascendancy in the state. Townley had been a highly successful flax grower for several years, but in 1912 he expanded operations too far, expecting to clear $100,000 while flaxseed was selling at $3 a bushel. Winter came much earlier than usual, ruining most of the crop. The price on the salvage fell to a dollar a bushel, and the flax king failed with liabilities of $80,000. It was then that he set out working for the Socialist Party and soon realized the effectiveness of touring the state in cheap automobiles and signing up the farmers as friends in a common cause. Then he decided to use the same method to organize them for socialistic ends by getting pledged candidates nominated in the Republican and Democratic conventions and primaries. In this way, some immediate gains could be made, but objectives without the underlying philosophy could not hold the farmers together once they reached their goal and began to feel easy again. Relaxed vigilance might all too soon wreck the whole scheme.

At first charging $2.50 a year, and then $6, Townley raised the membership fee to $9 after the election of 1915, on the theory that farmers would fight harder for a movement in which they had invested money. In seven months in 1915, he and his fellow organizers enrolled 22,000 members and set about capturing the conventions and primaries in the following spring. In this they were highly successful, and in the following November they elected Lynn J. Frazier as governor and all but one of the rest of the state officials, including William Langer as attorney general. Frazier won by a ratio of 4 to 1. Also they elected 81 out of 113 members of the lower house of the state legislature, but because 24 of the 49 members of the senate were holdovers, they fell a trifle short of controlling that body. In a special election in 1917, they also sent the cartoonist of their official newspaper, John M. Baer, to Congress and reelected him the next year. They passed a number of bills in the legislative session of 1917, with the support of a few of the holdover senators, but failed in a measure to draft a new state constitution.

In 1918 they retained the state offices, built up their strength in the supreme court to four out of the five judges, and got a wide control of both houses of the legislature. With this clear mandate, in 1919 the legislature enacted the entire League program, setting up five organizations: an Industrial Commission, a Bank of North Dakota, the North Dakota Mill and Elevator Association, the Home Building Association of North Dakota, and a comprehensive hail-insurance program. This put the state into the businesses of banking, the grading, storing, milling, and marketing of wheat, building houses, and insurance. Though the League made efforts to organize other states, the successes were quite limited. There was some activity in fifteen states, from Wisconsin to Washington and Texas, but Minnesota was the only state aside from North Dakota where membership was large, and it was not enough there to capture the government. Minnesota seated 7 League senators and 25 representatives as a result of the election of 1918. Idaho, with 8 senators and 14 representatives, ranked third, while the victory of United States Senator William E. Borah was with League support. Five senators and 13 representatives and the driving of Governor Peter Norbeck into liberal channels was a partial victory in South Dakota. A few legislative seats were gained also in Montana, Nebraska, and Colorado. By this time, the League had over 188,000 members, seven tenths of them paid-up. (*See Document No. 22.*)

There was another victory in North Dakota in 1920, but by reduced majorities. Frazier returned as governor; Edwin F. Ladd of the Agricultural College, who had been serving as state grain inspector, became a United States senator; and William Lemke succeeded Langer, who had deserted the League, as attorney general for the state. The electorate also accepted all League-initiated bills by ample majorities. In Minnesota, the vote was twice that of 1918, but the election of one representative to Congress was about the only material gain. In Wisconsin, the election of the governor, lieutenant governor, secretary of state, and five national representatives was really a victory for Robert M. La Follette, but the League also had supported the men. There were no other successful state tickets in this election, and the power of the organization seemed to be slipping at home. These were war years, and hysteria was sweeping the nation. Any program even faintly suggesting socialism was suspect. League leaders had been critical of the activities of the federal government and wanted to know why conscription of capital did not accompany that of cannon fodder. In 1921 Townley himself was jailed for ninety days on a trumped-up charge of sedition.

Furthermore, not all parts of the new legislation in North Dakota were working out to perfection. Under inexperienced management, the Bank of North Dakota was in troubled waters. The Home Building Association was bogging down, and the Mill and Elevator Association was slow in getting into motion. Businessmen were up in arms, while the farmers, never thoroughly indoctrinated and therefore disappointed at failure to see instantaneous miracles, began to drop out. Townley had spent too much effort in trying to capture state legislatures in distant parts and not enough in building up the League and in

consolidating his gains. The defection of Langer, of
Theodore G. ("Two-bit") Nelson of the Society of Equity,
and of others contributed to enfeeblement, while the
rise of the Farmer-Labor group in Minnesota drained
off membership into third-party action. In 1922 the
League lost control of the administration and legislature
in North Dakota, though sending Frazier to join Ladd
in the Senate, just as the Mill and Elevator Association
was proving a success, progressive taxation had justified
itself, and the hail, fire, and tornado insurance program
was flourishing.

The Farmer-Labor Party and the Nonpartisan
League. When in 1918 the League men failed to elect
Charles A. Lindbergh as governor, this started a movement for the creation of a new third party. In 1919 the
Minnesota Federation of Labor, looking with envy at the
successful labor policies in North Dakota, set up the
Working People's Nonpartisan League which was soon
followed by like groups in the Dakotas. In 1920 both
the labor and farmer groups backed Henrik Shipstead
for governor, but failed to elect him. In 1922 the Minnesota Farmer-Labor Party, now fully organized, elected
Shipstead to the Senate over the incumbent Frank B.
Kellogg, and when Knut Nelson died in the following
year, it sent Magnus Johnson to be the second senator.
Nonpartisan League support in both cases turned the
tide for the new party, and the same force was partly
responsible for the success of Burton K. Wheeler in his
senatorial race of 1922 in Montana. The League also
claimed credit for help in the election of Senators Smith
W. Brookhart in Iowa, R. B. Howell of Nebraska, and
Clarence C. Dill of Washington in the same year, but
proof is lacking that such support was the determining
factor in any of these cases. The same could be said for
responsibility for the election of ten representatives in
Congress from Wisconsin, seven from Oklahoma, two
from Nebraska, and one from Montana, or for the success of the gubernatorial candidates the Leaguers backed
in Wisconsin, Nebraska, Kansas, and Colorado. La Follette might well have carried the Wisconsin delegation
with no outside help. But claims for three representatives
from Minnesota and one from North Dakota are more
credible.

In 1924 the Farmer-Labor Party, along with the Socialists and the American Federation of Labor, supported La Follette for the Presidency, but he carried only his own state. In 1920, 1928, and 1932 the National Farmer-Labor Party had its own candidates for the Presidency, starting out with 265,000 votes for Parley P. Christensen of Utah and winding up with a little over 7,000 for the gallant old Jacob S. Coxey of Ohio, noted for his "industrial army" of 1894. William Lemke of the grossly heterogeneous Union Party of 1936 composed of followers of Francis E. Townsend, Charles E. Coughlin, and Gerald L. K. Smith, probably got a few Farmer-Labor votes also in his total of nearly 900,000. Certainly Lemke himself, who represented North Dakota in Congress from 1933 to 1939, had lost none of his old liberal fire. The Minnesota Farmer-Labor Party, which maintained independence of the national body and had not supported even Christensen, gained in strength for some years, re-electing the brilliant and courageous Governor Floyd B. Olson in 1934, and with him five of the nine representatives in Congress. In 1936 the Farmer-Labor Party of Minnesota, now combined with the Democrats, secured the largest majorities for its slate ever given to any party in that state. Liberal legislation had been in progress in Minnesota, but by this time it was largely in line with the New Deal policies of the federal government.

**The Farm Bloc.**  Though by 1922 the force of the Nonpartisan League was spent, not only had its display of power wrung concessions for the farmers from reluctant legislators trying to retain office in states where neither the League nor the Farmer-Labor Party was able to grasp the reins itself, but also the threat of further farm uprising stirred up action in Congress. Agriculture was, in fact, getting into a perilous condition just as the League was gasping for its last breath. The business of farming had prospered and expanded mightily after 1914, as a consequence of the war in Europe. The uprising in the northern part of the wheat belt was the outgrowth of local conditions that were hampering the growers from attaining their share of the general prosperity. America's entry into the conflict in 1917 brought multiplied activity, while prices kept ahead of soaring production. In 1918 the government had guaranteed the price of wheat at $2 a bushel, whereupon the crop increased two fifths in volume and yet was all needed. The Federal Farm Loan Banks, authorized by an act of 1916, aided in the extension of activities by encouraging the purchase of tractors and other improved implements and the increased use of fertilizers, while the Bureau of Markets reduced the threat of periodic gluts.

Then on May 31, 1920, government supports came off and prices dropped. The average acreage value of the ten leading crops in 1919 had been $35.74; in 1921, it was $14.45. The cost of farm purchases also had declined, but in a smaller degree. In the two years' time, the ratio of prices received to prices paid fell from 109 to 75 (base: 1910-1914 = 100). Wheat, corn, and the livestock industries suffered the most. In 1920 many farms in Iowa were changing hands at prices from $500 to $800 an acre, the buyers claiming they could make such values pay by raising onions at 15 cents a pound. All such land, thus utilized, would have produced enough onions to float the navies of the world in Irish stew, and the price of onions would probably be less than 15 cents a bushel. In the following summer when corn, the prevailing actual crop, dropped to 25 cents a bushel and farmers again began burning it for fuel, the land boom collapsed and speculators started shooting themselves or taking refuge in the asylums. Men with land mortgaged at $400 an acre, with the market value now down to $250, found it economical to let the banks foreclose and to make a new start on other farms just as good as the old. Five years later, when the long-term notes fell due, the banks had so much land worth less than the loans on it that they failed in swarms. It was a common thing in 1925 and 1926 to find county-seat cities that had not one bank left, while merchants were conducting business through small-town banks that had been too puny to help inflate the land bubble.

In proportion to American and world needs, there had been no actual overexpansion or excess production. Crops after the war were, in per capita and sometimes in actual amount, less than in the earlier years of the century. The corn of 1930 was a fifth less than in 1900. Wheat and corn had increased less than 42% in the 30 years, while population had grown 62%. All cereals in 1924 were below the yield of 1899, and the number of hogs and beef cattle in 1930 was less than in 1890, though population had almost doubled. The loss of foreign markets as the world settled down to production instead of destruction, a decline in domestic consumption, and the fact that half the people of the world could not buy what they needed to maintain a comfortable existence explained the presence of what was euphemistically called an "agricultural surplus." But farmers could not solve the problem of world distribution. What they knew was that they had been encouraged to buy expensive machinery, and to till more acres more intensively, and now, like the snipe hunter of old, they were left holding the bag far out in the economic wilderness, while general business, envisioned as the pranksters who had instigated the hunt, were safe back at home basking in the firelight of prosperity.

Conscious of this distress and discomfort at a time when farmer-labor combinations were threatening to take over the state governments of the Midwest, the new Farm Bureau Federation, fearing any radical plan that would iron out the differences between industrial and rural workers, began welding together a small group of ordinarily conservative members of Congress into a Farm Bloc. The first farm bureau was established at Binghamton, New York, in 1911, and hired an agent to supervise activities in Broome County. In the following year, the legislature of the state permitted counties to appropriate money for the employment of agents and for carrying out the farm-bureau work. The Smith-Lever Act of Congress, May 8, 1914, also provided for county agents, and a wartime act of August 10, 1917, authorized one for each county in the United States not already supplied. These agents set about organizing bureaus, and in 1919 the various state organizations scattered from New Hampshire to California established the national Farm Bureau Federation.

With James R. Howard and John W. Cloverdale of Iowa as president and secretary and Gray Silver of West Virginia as the head lobbyist at Washington, D. C., the Farm Bureau pursued zealously the postwar campaign against radicalism and worked hand-in-hand with the local chambers of commerce, banks, railroad officials, and

other business groups. Supplied also with funds from the
United States Department of Agriculture, here was an
organization that rapidly took on the big-business point
of view. Though the Bureau emphasized cooperative marketing and buying, it stressed farming as a business in
which the tactics of big business were the best. Tied in
with the Department of Agriculture and linked with the
state agricultural colleges, the Bureau was concerned
mainly with the interests of the greater and more opulent
farmers, took the view that there was no place in the
economy for the small operator, steadfastly resisted the
idea of local farm groups throwing their holdings together
for the more economical use of expensive equipment,
and looked upon the hired laborer only as a necessity for
the further advancement of the employer. The Iowa Farm
Bureau had organized in 1918 to prevent the invasion of
the Nonpartisan League, and had largely succeeded in
the effort.

By June 1, 1921, the Bureau had over a million members in 43 states, half of them in Iowa, Illinois, Ohio,
Texas, Michigan, and Indiana. Here was an organization
bent on objectives that old-line politicians could understand, and with a following large enough to command
respect. Perhaps the members could hold the balance of
power in a close election, and their demands were not of
the kind to disturb essentially the existing order. A little
backfiring with so moderate a group might well render
harmless the "political prairie fire" of the Nonpartisan
League. So, with Gray Silver supplying the timber, a
group of from 25 to 30 senators headed by William S.
Kenyon of Iowa, Arthur Capper of Kansas, and Ellison
D. Smith of South Carolina, and something over 90 representatives led by Lester J. Dickinson of Iowa, rolled logs
in Congress for a series of farm-relief measures in the
early 1920's. Their successes included an emergency tariff
in 1921, succeeded by the Fordney-McCumber Act of
1922, both of which were merely dust in the farmers'
eyes.

The revival of the War Finance Corporation, spending
over $433,000,000 to dump abroad surplus commodities
from thirty-seven states; an enlargement of the federal
land banks; the Packers and Stockyards Act; restrictions
on price manipulations; and a stiffened Grain Futures Act

were also accomplishments of 1921. The Clayton Anti-trust Act of 1914 had exempted farmers' cooperatives with no capital stock from prosecution, but a new measure of 1922 extended the immunity to such agencies when capitalized. As late as 1932 the Farm Bloc helped in the adoption of a much-needed Intermediate Credits Act. The dumping practices of the Finance Corporation brought forth foreign retaliation that nullified whatever slight benefits the new tariff may have gained. The other measures were all desirable, but they were not enough to cure the farm ills. A slight improvement came in 1924 and 1925, followed by almost continuous decline until 1932, when the ratio of prices received to prices paid reached 55.

Meanwhile, Senator Charles L. McNary of Oregon and Representative Gilbert N. Haugen of Iowa began in 1924 to present a series of bills for a new type of foreign dumping. The government should purchase the surpluses of wheat, corn, hogs, cotton, and tobacco, sell them abroad for what they would fetch, and assess the losses in the form of an equalization fee or debenture against the cooperating farm organizations. Frank O. Lowden, former governor of Illinois, declared it would be more economical to spill the products in the sea, since this would cause no reprisals. President Calvin Coolidge vetoed the bill in amended form when it passed Congress in 1927, thus putting the matter up to the voters in 1928. On June 15, 1929, following the triumph of Herbert C. Hoover, Congress provided for the setting up of a Federal Farm Board which got under way in the following month, the chairman being Alexander Legge of the International Harvester Company. The board created a Grain Stabilization Corporation, which in the next year bought and stored over 257,000,000 bushels of wheat, and a Cotton Stabilization Board, which in the same time acquired ownership of 1,300,000 bales. Yet prices continued to drop until wheat reached 25 cents a bushel and sometimes less and cotton was five cents a pound. Hoover advocated the withdrawal of land from cultivation, the plowing under of crops, and the slaughter of immature surplus meat animals, but nothing came of the recommendation until the next administration began offering bonuses for such destruction. In 1932 the Farmers' Union gave publicity to the failure of the whole program by pointing to thousands of farmers going into bankruptcy while the heads of the stabilization corporations were drawing salaries of $75,000 a year.

**The Farm-Holiday Movement.** Accelerated depression followed the Panic of 1929 and, along with the entire economy, brought farmers into deeper distress than ever before. In time the industrial laborer suffered more than all others, for the farmers could still raise something to eat. As one of them replied to this observation: "If things keep on like they are, just come back next year and you will find the fattest, sleekest, nakedest man you ever saw." Milo Reno, President of the Farmers' Union in Iowa, determined to avert this shock to the nation's aesthetic sensibilities. Born in 1866, interested in every farmers' movement since the heyday of the Grangers, joining the Farmers' Union in 1918, and becoming its Iowa leader in 1920, he soon became a power in the national organization. Reno was a man of varied gifts. An ordained preacher, in his lustier days he also had the reputation of being an accomplished fiddler and dancer, a lover of fast horses, a hard drinker, and a mighty wooer of the ladies. Now that he was growing old, he craved some real fun, to be obtained by applying the tactics of bankers, businessmen, and organized labor to the farm movement.

Bankers, faced with a run, had called a holiday. Business, confronted with low prices, had restricted output and withheld goods from the market. Labor, when milder measures failed, had struck. As early as 1920 Reno began urging such methods upon Iowa farmers, but for a long time they were unresponsive. They mistrusted industrial workers and were loath to copy the practices of labor unions. So, for a time, Reno centered his efforts on cooperative stores that often failed, gasoline filling stations that did somewhat better, and insurance companies that really flourished. But this was not enough. Farmers, especially after 1929, got steadily poorer. In 1931 three fifths of all Iowa farms were mortgaged, not for expansion purposes but simply to keep going. A seventh of the families had already suffered foreclosure and were reduced to tenancy or eviction. But Iowa was not alone in this dilemma; on one day of April in 1932, Mississippi sheriffs sold a quarter of the land in the state for satisfaction of mortgages and taxes.

By this time farmer resistance to strikes was breaking down. On May 3, 1932, some 3000 farmers assembled in Des Moines, at Reno's call, and elected him head of the National Farmers' Holiday Association, promising to withhold produce from the market until prices were right. But before this time the dairymen in Cedar County, birthplace of Hoover, had already risen in revolt, and the movement was spreading into neighboring counties. In 1928 they had celebrated the success of their favorite son who had gone out into the world and made good. But Hoover as President disappointed them and now they were bitter. Failing to see the ultimate benefits from compulsory testing of cows for tuberculosis, they realized only that the government did not pay adequately for slain beasts, and could not understand why the carcasses were fit for beef while the milk was contaminated. The Reno men pointed with glee to the national health champion who declared that she drank a quart of milk each day from a herd every cow of which, they learned, reacted positively to the tuberculin test. Something must be wrong with the whole procedure. In March, 1931, the Cedar County farmers began driving off, clubbing, or dunking in the horse trough the visiting state veterinarians and their police guards.

Acting as members of a Farmers' Protective Association, these twentieth-century Minute Men thus spared the Farmers' Union from complicity in any ensuing damage suits. Before this, Reno had surrendered control of the Iowa Union to a new president, but still was the power behind the administration. Following the first hostility, the testing program in that area lapsed for a few months while Governor Daniel W. Turner tried to work out a compromise short of the farmers' demand for a purely optional program. In September after the failure of this effort, Turner sent in the militia armed with tear gas. The farmers countered with their clubs, brickbats, and horse tanks. The superior force of the law won this Cedar County Cow War, and two of the rebels drew three-year prison sentences (but were paroled after four months). In time, most of the recalcitrants had to admit the validity of the tests and the long-term resulting

benefits. During the conflict Reno had remained in the
background, lending encouragement. (*See Document No. 23.*)

The major farm strike began in August, 1932, when
little of anything but eggs, milk, and hogs were moving to
the markets. The first action started with the Sioux City
Milk Producers' Association, in protest at two cents a
quart for milk delivered to the city and retailing at eight
cents. Frazier, Lemke, Langer, and Olson all favored the
protest, and there was some agitation in Illinois, Wisconsin, South Dakota, Nebraska, Kansas, and Montana.
But the main efforts were around Sioux City. Beginning
on August 11, members of the Producers' Association
pulled railroad ties and spiked planks across the roads to
stop milk trucks headed toward the city. Sometimes they
dumped the contents into the ditches, saving enough to
distribute free to needy citizens. They also stopped a few
trains hauling milk and livestock. Hogs were not getting
into Sioux City, but enough were reaching Chicago to
beat prices down. The Woodbury sheriff and a hundred
deputies were not enough to reopen traffic into Sioux
City. Iowa farmers, with help from the Nebraska side of
the line, also stopped hog shipments into Omaha. The
Pottawattamie County sheriff and fifty deputies used tear
gas and bullets to end the blockade of Council Bluffs and
on August 25 jailed forty-three rioters. A mob of 3000
was threatening a mass jail delivery when, to the relief of
the sheriff, a farmer pledged all of his unmortgaged property to bail them out. Two nights earlier, a sheriff's posse
had killed one and injured fourteen pickets, but the
sheriff and two of his deputies were acquitted of murder.
Reno then called a truce, but the farmers went ahead as
usual and as Reno had apparently expected. They carried
on a guerrilla campaign against the sheriffs' forces and on
one occasion ambushed four carloads of lawmen and
pummeled them distressfully.

The farm strike dwindled in intensity until the early
days of Franklin D. Roosevelt's administration, and then
it ceased, awaiting the action of the New Deal. The
change in control of the federal administration was helped
into being partly by farmers, infuriated by Vice-President
Charles Curtis when he told them they were "too damn
dumb" to understand the issues. Among the final activi-

ties of the embattled rustics were the "penny sales" that brought a final flicker of joy to the heart of Mary E. Lease, then on her deathbed. The plan worked best in Iowa, but also extended to Minnesota. Wherever a sheriff put a bankrupt farmer's real estate and chattels up for sale, his friends barred all other prospective purchasers and bid everything in at absurdly low prices, then returned them to the former owner as a permanent loan. After this had gone on for a while, farmers' "councils of defense" got creditors to scale down mortgages to an aggregate amount, according to the *New York Times,* of "hundreds of thousands of dollars." Some governors declared moratoriums of debts, and legislatures legalized the action. But foreclosures continued, and many thousands of families, bitter about past evictions, were out in November, 1932, to "get Hoover." The most astounding incident in the whole conflict occurred on April 23, 1933, when county judge Charles C. Bradley of Le Mars, Iowa, was dragged from his bench, with demands that he promise to sign no more orders for farm foreclosures. On his refusal, his captors slapped him around, hauled him out into the country, befouled him with transmission grease, and got him down on his knees to pray. They put a rope around his neck and desisted from hanging him only when he collapsed. (*See Document No. 24.*)

New Deal Relief.  It may be that such displays of determination and force had nothing to do with Roosevelt's prompt measures for agricultural relief, but his actions belie the assumption. The appointment of Henry A. Wallace of Iowa as Secretary of Agriculture was not wholly in recognition of his father's work in the Harding administration. Wallace well knew the situation where strife was hottest, and it seemed that he could cope with it. The legislation that followed seemed, for a time, to give a solution. The Farm Relief Act of May 12, 1933, assessed a tax on processers to use in paying farmers for limiting production of wheat, corn, hogs, dairy products, tobacco, cotton, and rice. When the Supreme Court overruled much of this law in January, 1936, Congress replaced it by payments for soil conservation. The Frazier-Lemke Act of 1934 provided a moratorium of five years on farm-mortgage foreclosures. In 1936, when the Supreme Court declared this a violation of due process,

Congress passed a slightly different measure that the Supreme Court approved after having been chastened by Roosevelt's threat of packing the bench.

While these and other measures were in operation, the ratio of farm prices received and paid rose to 92 in 1937, but it took another war to attain and exceed the level of 1919. The story of the New Deal does not properly belong to an account of farm movements, but it came as a culmination of them. Erratic as the activities of Townley and Reno may have been, they brought home to the politician a realization that the only way to prevent still more violent agrarian revolt was to give tender heed to the voice of rural protest. Since that time the farmer has been the darling of Democrats and Republicans alike, and his vote has been most sedulously courted. Many of the measures have been abortive in outcome; but since 1933, if the bed of the capitalist farmer has not always been strewn with roses, it is not because his voice has not been heard. During the early months of the New Deal, Reno continued his prodding. He called for a new farm strike to begin on October 31, 1933, and in a conference of governors induced Langer of North Dakota to place an embargo on wheat shipments. When this did not help prices, the Minute Men got to work again and burned a few railroad bridges to impede traffic. Then, in late November, Congress provided for the storage of wheat at a third more than its market price. Money began pouring in, and farm strikes ceased. Three years later, Reno died in a glow of triumph.

**The Problem of Hired Laborers and Tenants.** Now that the proprietary farmer had finally risen to political esteem, his future seemed to depend largely on his business acumen and his willingness to maintain a tight combination with all of his fellows in order to consolidate and retain his gains. By 1950 some 1,450,000—a quarter of all farm operators—belonged to the Farm Bureaus which were organized in nearly every state. The Grange had 850,000, largely in the East, and the Farmers' Union included 200,000 dues-paying members, mainly in the West and South. These national organizations, together with smaller groups, owned nearly 10,000 marketing and buying associations, with over 7,000,000 members distributed among all of the states, and doing an annual business of more than $8,000,000,000. Many farmers must have belonged to multiple associations, for there were only 5,382,000 farms in America. A million other farms had been absorbed by the more successful operators during the preceding thirty years. In the same time, farm population declined by 6,400,000. Of these, 5,500,000 had left in the last decade, leaving a bare 25,000,000 behind—1 in 6 of the total national population, a ratio which continued to decline. Thus was the city alleviating farm distress.

But another factor needs a brief consideration. Between 1945 and 1947, farm prosperity was at its peak. Yet in 1945 only 57% of farm operators owned their land outright; 11.3% were part owners, and 31.7% were tenants. At the same time, 9,844,000 persons were working on the land, of whom four tenths were neither owners nor tenants. Many of these were members of the families of operators, but 27% of all the rest were hired laborers. On this same larger basis of reckoning, 23% were tenants. A full half of the force, exclusive of families of operators, was sharing very slightly in prosperity.

Organization never went far among the hired hands. Before 1917 the Industrial Workers of the World enrolled migratory laborers in the West. They were efficient workers, but would tolerate no nonsense. Wages and working conditions had to be right or the harvest might go unthreshed. In 1917-1919, the socialistic and syndicalistic proclivities of the "Wobblies" made them easy victims of wartime hysteria. Hundreds received brutal treatment, and state legislation outlawed them. The I.W.W. continued to exist, but it dwindled to insignificance. Years passed before there were any further efforts at unionization. The New Deal was blissfully innocent of any concern for the farmer's hired hand, but spontaneous unions sprang up in 1933 and 1934, which the American Federation of Labor absorbed. They conducted some strikes in California and Ohio. First the Union of Mexican Field Workers and then the Cannery and Agricultural Workers' Industrial Union struck in the Imperial Valley for wages of as much as 35 cents an hour, whereupon "law and order" mobs conducted a reign of terror against them, beatings, abductions, and forcible ejections from the area being common events. In 1934 vigilantes burned the homes of Filipino strikers in the Salinas Valley and fired on them when they tried to save their property. Additional rage and gore suppressed a new effort in the Imperial Valley in 1935, and vigilante reprisals in the onion fields of Hardin County, Ohio, were almost as violent.

In the South the tenants and sharecroppers got nothing out of the Agricultural Adjustment Administration. Instead, the planters abandoned fields, turned their underlings out on the road, and collected the entire payments from the government for growing less cotton. With hordes of peons thus thrown on relief and the livelihood of the rest endangered by the consequent labor surplus, in 1934 a small group of Arkansas workers got a state charter for the Southern Tenant Farmers' Union. Not mainly because they invited some Socialists to give them guidance, but because they threatened the permanence of the color line by working, Negro and white together, in the same cause, the landlords rose in their wrath and might to suppress them. Southern industrialists shared the same zeal. "Divide and conquer" was the motto. The substitution of race for class would keep both blacks and whites in proper submissiveness. Arrests, evictions, beatings, and even murders were among the means employed to stamp out the movement. Yet as late as 1940 the Union retained 160 locals with 30,000 members, spread over several states, and had participated in many worthy causes. If there are to be farmers' movements in the future, they are likely to occur among the tenants and hired men. (*See Document No. 25.*)

# — 7 —

# SUMMARY AND CONCLUSIONS

There have been three and a half centuries of agriculture in America since the coming of the white man. During the colonial period the farmers' problems and movements grew out of greed in acquiring land, an archaic system of tenure, governmental meddling, and also, in the commercial phases of the business, the difficulty of fitting production to demand. With independence, new adjustments became necessary because of a shortage of money and the revenue needs of a new government. Feudal vestiges in land tenure caused some local troubles. But in the main, down to 1860 rapid expansion on a seemingly limitless frontier centered attention on a liberalization of the federal land policy, with some sporadic attention to the tariff, banking problems, and the development of means of transportation.

After the Civil War, commercialized agriculture having swept the country, the farmers found themselves victims of their own individualism. Though still for some time a majority of the population, their more aggressive mercantile, manufacturing, and banking rivals held control of economic affairs, and it required the rest of the century for the farmers to learn collective action. Before this time arrived, they were in the minority, yet were beginning to secure more attention. After 1933 farm owners no longer stood hat in hand at the servants' entrance, pleading for gratuities. Realizing at last that agriculturists can become most cantankerous, politicians went to great lengths to court their votes. The policies adopted as a result of this changed attitude were of less than face value. There was no real overproduction as long as much of the world was still hungry. Therefore, the political solutions brought about were the wrong approach to farm relief, and they did almost nothing for that half of the rural labor force that owned no land.

Also, the alleviation of the lot of the landholder came at the expense of the elimination of a vast number of small farmers. The Farm Bureau's theory may yet prevail. Agriculture may become just another big business, and farming as a way of life will be no more. It may be, as expounded by a prophet of calamity in 1933, that "The Farmer Is Doomed," at least the small farmer. But when the family-sized farm is gone and factory methods of production replace it, something vital to the American scene will also be lost.

# Part Two

## DOCUMENTS

# — Document No. 1 —

## OPECHANCANOUGH'S MASSACRE OF MARCH 22, 1622*

*John Smith, who wrote from the accounts of witnesses, gave as the immediate cause of the massacre the killing of Jack the Feather, a member of Opechancanough's tribe, by an Englishman in retaliation for the Indian's slaying of an Englishman named Morgan. Smith concluded with a summary of English reprisals and some of his personal comments of censure for lack of thoroughness in vengeance.*

At the losse of this Saluage, *Opechankanough* much grieued and repined, with great threats of reuenge; but the *English* returned him such terrible answers, that he cunningly dissembled his intent, with the greatest signes he could of loue and peace: yet within fourteene daies after he acted what followeth.

Sir *Francis Wyat* at his arriuall was aduertised, he found the Countrey setled in such a firme peace, as most men there thought sure and vnuiolable, not onely in regard of their promises, but of a necessitie. The poore weake Saluages being euery way bettered by vs, and safely sheltred and defended, whereby wee might freely follow our businesse: and such was the conceit of this conceited peace, as that there was seldome or neuer a sword, and seldomer a peece [gun], except for a Deere or Fowle; by which assurances the most plantations were placed straglingly and scatteringly, as a choice veine of the rich

* From John Smith, *General Historie of Virginia* (1624), as reprinted in Edward Arber, ed., *Capt. John Smith of Willoughby . . . , Works* (Birmingham, England, 1884), pp. 572-574, 584.

ground inuited them, and further from neighbours the better. Their houses generally open to the Saluages, who were alwaies friendly fed at their tables, and lodged in their bed-chambers; which made the way plaine to effect their intents, and the conuersion of the Saluages as they supposed.

Hauing occasion to send to *Opechankanough* about the middle of March, hee vsed the Messenger well, and told him he held the peace so firme, the sky should fall or he dissolued it; yet such was the treachery of those people, when they had contriued our destruction, euen but two daies before the massacre, they guided our men with much kindnesse thorow the woods, and one *Browne* that liued among them to learne the language, they sent home to his Master. Yea, they borrowed our Boats to transport themselues ouer the Riuer, to consult on the deuillish murder that insued and of our vtter extirpation, which God of his mercy (by the meanes of one of themselues conuerted to Christianitie) preuented; and as well on the Friday morning that fatall day, being the two and twentieth of March [April 7, N.S.], as also in the euening before, as at other times they came vnarmed into our houses, with Deere, Turkies, Fish, Fruits, and prouisions to sell vs: yea in some places sat downe at breakfast with our people, whom immediatly with their owne tooles they slew most barbarously, not sparing either age or sex, man woman or childe; so sudden in their execution, that few or none discerned the weapon or blow that brought them to destruction. In which manner also they slew many of our people at seuerall works in the fields, well knowing in what places and quarters each of our men were, in regard of their familiaritie with vs, for the effecting that great master-peece of worke their conuersion: and by this meanes fell that fatall morning vnder the bloudy and barbarous hands of that perfidious and inhumane people, three hundred forty seuen men, women and children; mostly by their owne weapons; and not being content with their liues, they fell againe vpon the dead bodies, making as well as they could a fresh murder, defacing, dragging, and mangling their dead carkases into many peeces, and carrying some parts away in derision, with base and brutish triumph. . . . [There follow, here, several pages of details.]

This lamentable and so vnexpected a disaster caused them all beleeue the opinion of Master *Stockam*, and draue them all to their wits end. It was twenty or thirty daies ere they could resolue what to doe, but at last it was concluded, all the petty Plantations should be abandoned, and drawne onely to make good fiue or six places, where all their labours now for the most part must redound to the Lords of those Lands where they were resident. Now for want of Boats, it was impossible vpon such a sudden to bring also their cattle, and many other things, which with much time, charge, and labour they had then in possession with them; all which for the most part at their departure was burnt, ruined and destroyed by the Saluages.

# — Document No. 2 —

# INCIDENTS IN THE PEQUOT WAR, 1636-1637*

*One of the English leaders of the Pequot War, John Underhill, the "good fighter, but a sorry scamp" mentioned in Chapter 1 above, gives some details of John Endecott's provocative raid in 1636 and the massacre of the Pequots in their fort on the Mystic River on May 20, 1637.*

The last messenger brought us this intelligence from the sachem, that if we would but lay down our arms, and approach about thirty paces from them, and meet the heathen prince, he would cause his men to do the like, and then we shall come to a parley.

* From John Underhill, "Nevves from America" (London, 1638), in *Massachusetts Historical Society Collections,* 3d Series, Vol. VI (Boston, 1837), pp. 10-11, 24-25.

But we seeing their drift was to get our arms, we rather chose to beat up the drum and bid them battle. Marching into a champaign field we displayed our colors; but none would come near us, but standing remotely off did laugh at us for our patience. We suddenly set upon our march, and gave fire to as many as we could come near, firing their wigwams, spoiling their corn, and many other necessaries that they had buried in the ground we raked up, which the soldiers had for booty. Thus we spent the day burning and spoiling the country. Towards night embarked ourselves. The next morning, landing on the Nahanticot shore, where we were served in like nature, no Indians would come near us, but run from us, as the deer from the dogs. But having burnt and spoiled what we could light on, we embarked our men, and set sail for the Bay. Having ended this exploit, came off, having one man wounded in the leg; but certain numbers of theirs slain and many wounded. This was the substance of the first year's service. . . .

Most courageously these Pequeats behaved themselves. But seeing the fort was too hot for us, we devised a way how we might save ourselves and prejudice them. Captain Mason entering into a wigwam, brought out a firebrand, after he had wounded many in the house. Then he set fire on the west side, where he entered; myself set fire on the south end with a train of powder. The fires of both meeting in the centre of the fort, blazed most terribly, and burnt all in the space of half an hour. Many courageous fellows were unwilling to come out, and fought most desperately through the palisadoes, so as they were scorched and burnt with the very flame, and were deprived of their arms—in regard the fire burnt their very bowstrings—and so perished valiantly. Mercy they did deserve for their valor, could we have had opportunity to have bestowed it. Many were burnt in the fort, both men, women, and children. Others forced out, and came in troops to the Indians, twenty and thirty at a time, which our soldiers received and entertained with the point of the sword. Down fell men, women, and children; those that scaped us, fell into the hands of the Indians that were in the rear of us. It is reported by themselves, that there were about four hundred souls in this fort, and not above five of them escaped out of our hands. Great and doleful was the bloody sight to the view of young soldiers that never had been in war, to see so many souls lie gasping on the ground, so thick, in some places, that you could hardly pass along.

— Document No. 3 —

# COLONIAL ATTITUDES ON KING PHILIP'S WAR, 1675-1676*

*Increase Mather published an account of King Philip's War in 1676. His son Cotton Mather, who was thirteen and a half years old when Philip died, also wrote about the same events some years later. The rather stern attitudes of these two Congregational ministers reflect the contempt and fear of the Indians held by the colonists of that day. Only the imputed causes and the account of the death of Philip will be repeated here.*

As for the Grounds, Justness, and Necessity of the present *War* with these Barbarous Creatures which have set upon us, my design is not to *inlarge* upon that Argument, but to leave that to others whom it mostly concerns, only in brief this. The irruption of this flame at this time was occasioned as followeth.

In the latter end of the Year 1674. An *Indian*, called *John Sausaman*, who had submitted himself unto, and was taken under the protection of the *English*, perceiving that the *profane Indians* were hatching mischief against

* From Increase Mather, *The History of King Philip's War;* Cotton Mather, *A History of the Same War* (Boston, 1862), pp. 47-54, 193-195.

the *English*, he faithfully acquainted the Governour of *Plymouth*, with what he knew, and also what his fears were, together with the grounds thereof, withal declaring; that he doubted such and such *Indians*, belonging to *Philip* the Sachem of *Pokanoket* or *Mount-hope*, would murder him; which quickly happened accordingly: For soon after this, *John Sausaman* was barbarously murdered by an *Indian*, called *Tobias* (one of *Philip's* chief Captains and Counsellors) and by his son and another *Indian*, who knocked him on the head and then left him on the Ice on a great Pond. . . . An *Indian* unseen by those three that killed Sausaman, beheld all. . . . The three *Indians* who had committed the murder were apprehended. . . . They had a fair Tryal for their Lives, and . . . *Indians* as well as *English* sate upon the *Jury*, and all agreed to the condemnation of those Murtherers. . . .

No doubt but one reason why the *Indians* murdered *John Sausaman*, was out of hatred against him for his Religion, for he was Christianized and baptiz'd, and was a Preacher amongst the *Indians* . . . but the main ground why they murthered him seems to be, because he discovered their subtle and malicious designs, which they were complotting against the *English*. *Philip* perceiving that the Court of *Plymouth* had Condemned and Executed one of his Counsellors, being (as is upon strong grounds supposed) conscious of the murder committed upon *John Sausaman*, must needs think that ere long, they would do to him (who had no less deserved it) as they had done to his Counsellor: Wherefore he, contrary to his Covenant and Faith engaged to *Plymouth* Colony, yea, and contrary to his promise unto some in this Colony (for about five years ago, *Philip* made a disturbance in *Plymouth* Colony, but was quieted . . . when he engaged, that if at any time hereafter he should think the *English* among whom he lived did him wrong, he would not cause any disquietment before such time as he had acquainted the *English* of *Mattachusets*, but contrary to these solemn engagements he) doth call his Men together and *Arm* them, and refused to come when sent for, by the Authority of *Plymouth*, unto whose Government he had subjected himself. Hereupon the *English* in *Plymouth* Jurisdiction, sent a small Army to those Towns next *Mount hope*, in order to reducing *Philip* to his obedience, and for the security

of those places which were in great danger, and in no less
fear, by reason of the insolency of the Heathen. . . .

August 12 [1676]. This is the memorable day wherein
*Philip,* the perfidious and bloudy Author of the War and
wofull miseryes that have thence ensued, was taken and
slain. And God brought it to pass, chiefly by *Indians*
themselves. For one of *Philips* men (being disgusted at
him, for killing an *Indian* who had propounded an expedient for peace with the *English*) ran away from him,
and coming to Road-Island, informed that *Philip* was
now returned again to *Mount-Hope,* and undertook to
bring them to the Swamp where he hid himself. Divine
Providence so disposed, as that Capt. *Church* of *Plymouth*
was then in Road-Island, in order to recruiting his
Souldiers, who had been wearied with a tedious march
that week. But immediately upon this Intelligence, he set
forth again, with a small company of *English* and *Indians.*
It seemeth that night *Philip* (like the man, in the Host of
*Midian*) dreamed that he was fallen into the hands of
the *English,* and just as he was saying to those that were
with him, that they must fly for their lives that day, lest
the *Indian* that was gone from him should discover where
he was. Our Souldiers came upon him and surrounded
the *Swamp* (where he with seven of his men absconded)
Thereupon he betook himself to flight; but as he was
coming out of the Swamp, an *English-man* and an *Indian*
endeavoured to fire at him, the *English-man* missed of his
aime, but the *Indian* shot him through the heart, so as
that he fell down dead. The *Indian* who thus killed *Philip,*
did formerly belong to Squaw-Sachim of *Pocasset,* being
known by the name of *Alderman.* In the beginning of the
war, he came to the Governour of *Plymouth,* manifesting
his desire to be at peace with the *English,* and immediately
withdrew to an Island not having engaged against the
*English* nor for them, before this time. Thus when *Philip*
had made an end to deal treacherously, his own Subjects
dealt treacherously with him. This Wo was brought upon
him that spoyled when he was not spoyled. And in that
very place where he first contrived and began his mischief,
was he taken and destroyed, and there was he (like as
Agag was hewed in pieces before the Lord) cut into four
quarters, and is now hanged up as a monument of reveng-
ing Justice, his head being cut off and carried to *Plymouth,*

his Hands were brought to *Boston. So let all thine Enemies perish, O Lord!* When *Philip* was thus slain, five of his men were killed with him, one of which was his chief Captains son, being (as the *Indians* testifie) that very *Indian* who shot the first gun at the *English,* when the War began. So that we may hope that the War in those parts will dye with *Philip.*

— Document No. 4 —

# COMMUNICATION FROM QUITRENT RIOTERS AROUND NEWARK, N. J., 1746*

*The following letter appeared in the* New York Post-Boy *of February 17 [O.S.], 1745-6, in reply to an account of the riot published in the same newspaper four weeks earlier. In June of the same year, J. Zenger (seemingly the John Peter Zenger of the famous freedom-of-the-press trial of 1734-1735) published an open letter in New York on the same lines, but much less comprehensive. John Peter Zenger died in the following month.*

Mr. Parker,

Divers Persons having seen in your Post-Boy of January 20th, an Account of an extraordinary Riot at Newark, &c. touching three Persons committed to Jail, whereof one was Nehemiah Baldwin, who it is said, *offered to give Bail; pursuant unto which the Sheriff was about carrying*

* From William A. Whitehead, ed., *Archives of the State of New Jersey,* 1st Series, Vol. VI (Newark, 1882), pp. 292-295.

*him to the Judge, &c.* This matter is not put in a true
Light; The said Baldwin, as well as the other two, had
Offer made by the Sheriff, if they would give Bail, they
might all be discharged; to which they all refused. And
as is further said, *a great Number of People appearing
with Cudgels from the back Settlements, &c.* Take the
reply, in the following Narative, containing and setting
forth the Reasons why People were so exasperated.
Whereas sundry of the Proprietors, so called, had in the
late Years of 43, and 44, sent about and surveyed almost
all the unimproved Lands in the Country of Essex, with
a great Number of Improvements and settled Plantations,
particularly above the Mountain to Passaick River, including Mr. Van Gesin's Purchase, so called, and all
Horseneck Purchase, with the Improvements and Settlements, to the Number of three or four Score Plantations
and Families, &c. who in the general, having bought their
Lands of or from the native Owners and Proprietors of
the same, and possessed it, many of them some Scores of
Years, tho't their Properties secure from any Invasion;
when said Proprietors, so called, selling some of the Lands
surveyed as aforesaid, and offering the rest to Sale; and
withal serving several Ejectments on the Long possessed
as aforesaid, threatening to dispossess one and all, who
would not yield their Right and comply with their un-
reasonable Demands; and moreover to make all Persons
in said County and Country, who had Patents, &c. pay to
them Quit-Rents, to the Value of 30 or 40,000 Pounds,
&c. These things so animated the People to stand by and
for their Rights, Privileges and Properties, that in order
to secure and defend them in a due regular Manner, they,
in February, 1744, chose a Committee to act for them, in
such Negotiations as might be thought proper, to transmit
their Affairs and Circumstances home to England, and
lay them before His Majesty King George in Council, &c.
Upon this motion or Design manifested, said Proprietors
reduplicate their Processes by Ejectments, &c. The Committee aforesaid, March 27th, sent several of their
Number to wait on Mr. O[gde]n (a Person concerned in
the Affairs relating to *Horseneck, &c.*) who offered, if
they would pleased to take any one or two particular
Cases relating to said purchase (or any other they had by
Delegation Concern in & for) they would join Issue with

them in the Law for a Trial; in consideration they might have Liberty of appeal home to England, if Occasion offered, &c. and the like Proposal or Offer was made again by Messrs J[oh]n L[o]w, Esq: and J[oh]n C[ondi]t, in the Name of the Committee, to Messrs. A[lexande]r, M[orri]s, and O[gde]n Esqrs. at Perth Amboy, when sent thither to treat with them on that Affair; But, in short, all their Proposals were rejected, and they return, with this Declaration, viz. That they would not stop their Processes for two, three, nor yet ten Cases of Actions, if they were answered in the Law, &c. Afterward came a Proposal or Offer, from Mr. O[gde]n to said Committee, viz. of making or giving them Allowance of Eighteen Months for effecting the Business on foot, relating to the Purchases; in Consideration said Committee would become obliged to deliver up all the purchased Lands and Possessions they laid Claim unto, into their Hands at the Expiration or said Term of 18 Months, if their Purchases of Grants were not then established. To which, Reply was made, that in Case they complied with said Proposals, &c. would they be obliged to make a Redelivery of the Premises, if after said Term limitted, the purchased Rights should be established or confirmed at home? to which Mr. O[gde]n answered negatively. Soon after which they began again the Invasion of Men's Rights, Properties and Possessions: For one Samuel Baldwin having been for many Years possessed of Land lying within Van Gesin's Grant, or Purchase aforesaid (which the Proprietors had surveyed as above) and (as he was wont) cutting some Logs thereon for his Saw-Mill, &c. they arrested him to the Supream Court, put him in Jail, and made 30 or 40 Writs more, (as it was said) to serve on Men, for such like Trespasses, as they call 'em. This Baldwin being one of the Committee aforesaid, the rest of that Number determined to bail him, and stand Trial, &c. But the People in general supposing the Design of the Proprietors was to ruin them (which they well knew, should they prosecute and succeed according to their Threats, &c. would be the Consequence) and by Multiplicity of Law-Suits and Expence, thereby to impoverish and weaken them, that they should not be able to prosecute their Design (of sending home) to Effect; and withal, supposing they could not live under such Oppressions, which, (as it is said)

*makes wise Men mad;* they went to the Prison, opened
the Door, took out Baldwin, and returned peaceably,
ordering the Breach made to be well mended: which was
done accordingly. *Note,* The Ground of the above Sup-
position (besides what has been offered) was this; a
certain Gentleman of the adverse Party, discoursing con-
cerning a certain bill to be exhibited in Chancery, relating
to their Affairs with Elizabeth Town; declared, if they
could once make their Matters bear, to bring in said Bill;
it would put a Stop to Elizabeth Town's Proceeding, by
Reason the Expence would be so great, they could never
take it out, &c. Thus you have a brief Hint of the Grounds
or Causes why People have been so exasperated: We will
only add in a word what some of us has met with, set
forth as a Reason for their sending home, viz. That the
Invasion of our just Rights, Properties and Possessions, in
and by the Oppressions and Frauds of the Proprietors, so
called, is the only Spring of our Motion in the Matter of
Complaint offered; it being notoriously known, how they
impose upon, or rather deceive and beguile innocent,
weak and ignorant Men, many and diverse Ways; and
that when or after they, or some of them, have sold Lands
to Persons under Colour of Right, &c. others under the
like Pretence of Proprietie, have again, or afterwards, sold
the same lands; whereby the Purchasers are not only
frauded, but even the whole Country is in Confusion.

## — Document No. 5 —

# NATHANIEL BACON'S VERSION OF HIS REBELLION*

*The account by Mrs. Bacon (née Mary Horsmanden)
comes first, though dated a few days later than that of her*

* From "Bacon's Rebellion: Eggleston MSS," *William and
Mary College Quarterly Historical Magazine,* Vol. IX
(July, 1900), pp. 4-10.

*husband. The form of abbreviation then in use is some-*
*times confusion until one gets acquainted with it, espe-*
*cially as the letter y substitutes for th—the, that, and them*
*appearing as y^e, y^t, and y^m, but being pronounced as*
*though fully spelled out. The meanings of other abbrevi-*
*ations are rather obvious.*

✓            ✓            ✓

*A copy of Mrs. Bacon's letter . . . in Virginia, June*
*y^e 29th, 76, sent to her sister, & received the 26^th of*
*September, 1676. . . .*

DEAR SISTER,

I pray God keep the worst Enemy I have from ever
being in such a sad condition as I have been in since my
former to the: occasioned by y^e troublesome Indians, who
have killed one of our Overseers at an outward plantation
which wee had, and we have lost at great stock of cattle,
which wee had upon it, and a good crop that wee should
have made there, such plantation Nobody durst come
nigh, which is a very great losse to us.

If you had been here, it would have grieved your heart
to hear the pitiful complaints of the people, the Indians
killing the people daily the Govern: not taking any notice
of it for to hinder them, but let them daily doe all the
mischief they can: I am sure if the Indians were not
cowards, they might have destroied all the upper plantations, and killed all the people upon them; the Governour so much their friend, that hee would not suffer
any body to hurt one of the Indians; and the poor people
came to your brother to desire him to help against the
Indians, and hee being so much concerned for the losse
of his Overseer, and for the losse of so many men and
women and children's lives every day, hee was willing to
doe them all the good hee could; so hee begged the
Governour for a commission in severall letters to him,
that hee might goe out against them, but hee would not
grant one, so daily more mischief done by them, so your
brother not able to endure any longer, he went out without a commission. The Govern^r being very angry with
him put out high things against him, and told mee that
he would most certainly hang him as soon as hee returned,
w^ch hee would certainly have done; but what for fear of

the Governour's hanging him, and what for fear of the
Indians killing him brought mee to this sad condicion, but
blessed be God hee came in very well, with the losse of
a very few men; never was known such a fight in Virginia
with so few men's losse. The fight did continue nigh a
night and a day without any intermission. They did
destroy a great many of the Indians, thanks bee to God,
and might have killed a great many more, but the Govern^r
were so much the Indians' friend and our enemy, that hee
sent the Indians word that Mr. Bacon was out against
them, that they might save themselves. After Mr. Bacon
was come in hee was forced to keep a guard of soldiers
about his house, for the Govern^r would certainly have
had his life taken away privately, if hee would have had
opportunity; but the country does so really love him,
that they would not leave him alone any where; there was
not any body against him but the Govern^r and a few of
his great men, which have gott their Estates by the
Govern^r; surely if your brother's crime had been so great,
all the country would not have been for him, you never
knew any better beloved than hee is. I doe verily believe
that rather than hee should come to any hurt by the
Governour or any body else they would most of them
willingly loose their lives. The Govern^r has sent his Lady
into England with great complaints to the King ag^t Mr.
Bacon, but when Mr. Bacon's and all the people's complaints be also heard, I hope it may be very well. Since
your brother came in hee hath sought to the Govern^r for
commission, but none would be granted him, so that y^e
Indians have had a very good time, to doe more mischief.
They have murdered and destroied a great many whole
families since, and the men resolving not to goe under
any but yo^r brother, most of the country did rise in
Armes, and went down to the Govern^r, and would not
stirr till hee had given a commission to yo^r brother w^ch
hee has now done. He is made Generall of the Virginia
Warr, and now I live in great fear, that hee should loose
his life amongst them. They are come verry nigh our
Plantation where wee live.

*Mr. Bacon's acct of their troubles in Virginia by y^e
Indians, June y^e 18^{th}, 1676.*
By an Act of State it was pvided for y^e better security

of the country, That no Trade should be held with y^e
Indians, notw^th standing w^ch our present Govern^r monopolized a trade w^th y^e Indians & granted licences to others
to trade w^th y^m for w^ch hee had every 3^rd skinne, which
trading w^th y^e Indians has proved soe fatall to these pts
of y^e world, y^t I feare wee shall bee all lost for this commerce having acquainted y^e Indians o^r neighbours, but
most inveterate Enemy w^th our manner of living and
disipline of warr; has also brought them generally to y^e
use of o^r Fire Arms w^th such dexterity, y^t o^rselves often
hire y^m to kill Deare; & they have allmost lost y^e use of
their bowes and arrows, & every body through connivance
have for luc^re sake supplied y^m w^th ammunition (though
a prohibited commodity) y^t they have been in a condition
to punish us.

Things standing in this posture, they have entered into
generall bloody warr w^th all these pts of y^e world, y^e murders and depradations they have committed here are
horrible and continuall, laying a great part of y^e country
desolate, and forcing the inhabitants to fly from theire
dwellings to their ruine; y^e Govern^r (who from y^e Neigh-
bo^r Indians receives this Tribute & benefit by y^e trade)
still ptecting y^m for these many years ag^t y^e people, &
tho. y^e complaints of their murd^rs have been continuall
yett hee hath connived at y^e great men's furnishing y^m
with ammunition (w^ch by y^e Law is death), and y^e sad
effects thereof. Now y^e Govern^r having placed mee here
in a place of trust, I thought it my duty to discharge my
conscience in it, by introducing a looking after y^e wellfare
of the people here, they being poor, few and in scattered
habitations on y^e Frontiers & remote pt of y^e country,
nigh these Indians, who falling upon us (as well as other
pts) & killing amongst y^e rest, my Overseer and laying
desolate a plantation of mine to my great lose of cattle &
all my crop: I sent to y^e Govern^r for a commission to fall
upon y^m, but being from time to time denied, and finding
y^t y^e country was basely for a small and sordid gain be-
traied, & y^e lives and fortunes of y^e poor inhabitants
wretchedly sacrificed, resolved to stand up in this ruinous
gap; & rath^r expose my life and fortune to all hazards,
than basely desert my post, & by soe bad an example
make desolate a whole country, in w^ch no one dared to
stirr ag^t y^e common Enemy, but came flying from y^e

Enemy and crowded together like sheep, leaving their plantations and stock a prey to y^e Enemy.

Upon this I resolved to march out upon the Enemy w^th w^t volunteers I could y^n gett, but by soe doing found y^t I not onely lost y^e Governour's favour, but exposed my verry life and fortune at home as well as abroad; for y^t hee tho^u by mee and others often humbly requested, would by no means consent to my going out, being most unwilling y^t point should bee handled, w^ch had been so long concealed; but considering y^e necessity, I still pceeded, & returned w^th a greater victory from sharper conflict than ever yett has been known in these pts of the world; for y^t w^th about 70 men onely w^ch engaged and stood by me (y^e service being too hott for y^e rest) we fell upon a town of y^e Indians, consisting of 3 forts strongly mann'd, beginning our fight after midnight close at their port holes, & maintained it so all y^e remainder of y^e night, & in y^t time burnt their king's forts, & all theirin. The fight continued till y^e next day about 3 or 4 in y^e afternoon w^thout ceasing, in w^ch time their king making a sally was killed w^th most of his men, soe y^t wee reckned, wee destroyed about 100 men and 2 of their kings, besides women & children. This victory being y^e greatest & ag^t 2 of their most valiant nations gave great satisfaction to y^e people, but so enraged y^e Govern^r y^t I came home with greater danger y^n I went out, for being putt out of y^e Councell, I was chosen by y^e country a Burgesse, but going down in my sloop was seized on, & my fellow Burgesse putt in irons: but immediately all y^e country was in armes for my relief, such an appearance as has not been known in Virginia, threatening y^e ruine of all if any thing were done to my prejudice, who had so freely stood up in their defence, upon w^ch by y^e importunity of my cousin, & to shew my cleanesse from any ill intencons as also to reconcile y^e people and the Govern^r, who found my party too universall, & himself left w^th none but his Councell, y^e people generally disaffecting his pceedings, hee resolved imediately for England; unlesse I to salve his hon^r would submitt, & doe soe generous an Act (as my cozen formed it) as to acknowledge y^t my actions were unjust & unwarrantable, to beat up drums w^thout y^e Govern^rs leave, w^ch if I should doe, all should be well; whereupon I followed his advice not suspecting y^e pfidious hatred of y^e

Govern$^r$, who yett restored mee upon this to y$^e$ Councell, granted mee his pardon as fully as any ever was granted, and by one of the Burgesses proclaimed mee Generall to satisfy and disperse y$^e$ people, who were so satisfied herew$^{th}$ y$^t$ they all retired peaceably, but hee brok his word, & refused to signe my comission, w$^{ch}$ y$^e$ people highly resented, expecting y$^e$ pformance of his word, & univ$^r$sally resolving to goe und$^r$ no other man; & thereupon all y$^e$ country immediately up in arms & their heat increasing by y$^e$ repetition of y$^e$ sad and bloody murthers just at o$^r$ doors for wee are surrounded w$^{th}$ nations of Indians on all sides, except y$^e$ seaboard side of Virgin$^a$, so many y$^t$ none can guess at their number, who are now if not all a vast numb$^r$ of them confederated, & have for some time been in open wars w$^{th}$ us: y$^e$ stage and seat of y$^e$ war being now, & has for some time, nigh my doors, for you know S$^r$ I have formerly intimated my vicinity to them, & y$^t$ as others did so I also had a mind to look into y$^e$ gainfulnesse of trading w$^{th}$ them. Till I saw into y$^e$ fatall consequences thereof to y$^e$ country, w$^{ch}$ made mee become y$^e$ Indians' Enemy, who have only use y$^e$ trade to furnish themselves w$^{th}$ instrum$^{ts}$ to destroy vs; you would wonder to see y$^e$ sad condition wee are in: y$^e$ Indians being every where seen, y$^e$ houses & plantacons Deserted, and all left a prey to y$^e$ Enemy, till w$^{th}$in 3 miles of my dwelling, yet no man dared to stir or endeavor to destroy y$^e$ Indians because some of y$^m$ whom y$^e$ Govern$^r$ and those licensed by him trade w$^{th}$, are under his ptection, tho$^u$ we find y$^m$ all alike, neither can we distinguish this fatall undistinguishable distinction of y$^e$ Govern$^r$, who only for y$^e$ gain sake has bridled all people, y$^t$ no man dare to destroy y$^e$ Indians, even in y$^e$ psuit of murder untill I adventured to cutt y$^e$ knott, w$^{ch}$ made y$^e$ people in generall look upon mee as y$^e$ countries friend; for y$^t$ no man could pceive in my manner, Estate, or manner of living, how any indirect end, as levelling or rebellion, could make me desirous to exchange my fortune for worse; altho by the Govern$^r$ & some other of his creatures, such terms were putt upon mee, and y$^e$ Govern$^r$ being much incenced, and jealous of y$^e$ people's inclinations to mee, resolved after y$^e$ people were quietly dismissed, not only to deny my comission, but to take mee: and for the former, upon my serv$^{ts}$ report y$^t$ he saw an Indian in y$^e$ way, y$^e$ Govern$^r$ caused him to bee imprison'd & endeavoured to psuade y$^e$ house y$^t$ this report was only a plott to amuse y$^e$ people, & tho y$^e$ house gave little credence to y$^e$ Govern$^{rs}$ story, yet he took occasion from hence, not to signe my commission, upon w$^{ch}$ I desired his permission to goe home, & took a civill leave, but hee taking y$^e$ advantage of my late departure, caused mee to be besett both by water, and land, w$^{th}$ a designe to murder mee, w$^{ch}$ a friend of mine acquainted mee w$^{th}$. I took y$^e$ next horse, and went away alone. I was noe sooner gone but psued and searched for. They feeling the very beds for mee, seized on my Servants in Town, imprisoned them, but finding y$^t$ I was gone they were dismissed. Vpon my return home without a comission, this strange disappointment of y$^e$ people, putt all in armes again, in w$^{ch}$ posture they went down to Town to expect y$^e$ pformance of y$^e$ Govern$^{rs}$ promise, who then confirmed to y$^e$ people their desire, and has sent to England to acquaint his Ma$^{ty}$ of y$^e$ reasons and grounds of our distraccons & of his being now satisfied of my intentions, as you will further understand by his letter directed to his Ma$^{ty}$ from y$^e$ Governour and grand assembly. How long this fair weather will last I cannot tell, but doe earnestly desire wee may have so fair a representation in England, as y$^e$ countries complaints may be audited, either by agents from hence to England or there by comm$^{rs}$ from thence: & his Ma$^{ty}$ & y$^e$ world will quickly pceive how y$^e$ case stands between the Governour, and the country.

S$^r$ I am at present engaged in providing for safety of y$^e$ country, in all pts, having y$^e$ care of y$^e$ warre upon my hands; therefore I hope you will please to pardon my manner of Writing &c$^a$.

— Document No. 6 —

# GRIEVANCES OF THE NORTH CAROLINA REGULATORS, 1765-1771*

*The complaints of colonial farmers, more than of those in later periods, were against the tyranny of the law, of public officials from governors down to local satraps, and, in the case of the Regulators, of the lawyers. But quite like the Populists of the 1890's, they also protested against inequitable taxation and a shortage of money. Deviating from the general practice in these documents, the following excerpts are from a secondary monograph, written during the period of the Populist upheaval.*

↗          ↗          ↗

The grievances of the Regulators were excessive taxes, dishonest sheriffs, and extortionate fees. Each of these was made more intense by the scarcity of money. The stamp-act trouble does not seem to have had any immediate influence on this movement. That the people of the back country sympathized with the Sons of Liberty and could have been aroused to help them had the discontent spread from the Cape Fear inward is undoubtedly true, but this whole movement passed over before the Regulation came into existence.

The charge of excessive taxation was only relatively true. Taxes were apportioned by the poll. . . . This injustice was emphasized as between the east and the west by the fact that the wealthy gentlemen of the former section relied on slave labor, while slaves were comparatively few in the west.

The manner of collecting taxes made the burden still

* From John Spencer Bassett, "The Regulators of North Carolina (1765-1771)," *American Historical Association Annual Report, 1894* (Washington, 1895), pp. 150-155.

heavier. The tax bills, although questioned by the Regulators, seem to have been correct. In a frontier region, where money was scarce and local trading was confined almost entirely to barter, it was not always convenient for the farmers to keep money in their homes. But throughout the country there were men who lent small sums to the countrymen when there was a sudden demand for cash. Consequently, when the sheriff would come unexpectedly to the taxpayer, the latter would propose to get the money if the officer would accompany him to the home of this neighborhood banker. The officer usually refused to do this and proceeded to distrain on some property, taking a fee of 2s. 8d, for the same. The taxpayer would then hasten to his neighbor's, secure the needed money, and hurry after the sheriff. That officer would take a different route than the one he had promised to take, and the luckless pursuer would arrive in Hillsboro in time to see his property sold to some friend of the officer's for much less than its value. The Regulators charged that officers played into each other's hands for this purpose, and that there were men in Hillsboro who had made large sums by dealing in such business.

The sheriffs were thought to have taken another step in defiance of popular justice when the assembly in 1768 passed a law requiring the sheriffs to attend five different places in each county, at least two days in each place, during January and February of each year, in order to collect the taxes. If the officer found it necessary to call at the home of the ratepayer for his due, he took an extra fee for doing it. . . .

Another very prominent grievance was the dishonesty of the sheriffs who failed to pay into the hands of the public treasury the money they had collected. The public accounts were most inefficiently kept. There was a prevalent opinion among all classes that there was fraud just here. In 1767 Governor Tryon declared it as his opinion that "the sheriffs have embezzled more than one-half of the public money ordered to be raised and collected by them". . . .

Extortionate fees were perhaps the greatest grievance of all. Nearly all the officers were paid in fees. The people of the back counties complained heavily of their officers, and in support of their complaint the Orange

County Regulators produced affidavits sufficient to satisfy the most skeptical that they were right. As soon as counties were organized on the frontier sheriffs, clerks, registers, and lawyers swooped down upon the defenseless inhabitants like wolves. Further than this, the people charged that the superior and county courts conspired to aid the officers in escaping punishment. The fee of a lawyer was fixed by law, but like usury laws of our own day, it was difficult to enforce this law. . . .

Connected with and influencing each of these grievances was that of the general scarcity of money. The English colonial policy had the effect of withdrawing from the colonies as much gold and silver as possible. So scarce did this money become that in 1765 Governor Tryon said that there was only enough of it in the colony to pay for the stamps which under the Stamp Act would be required on the instruments of writing used in one year in the superior courts of the province. The people desired to issue a paper currency sufficient in amount for the demands, but were restrained by an act of Parliament made for the protection of British merchants, which forbade the colonies to issue legal-tender paper. The assembly petitioned the King for a relaxation of this injunction, but was unsuccessful. Distress was everywhere; but in the east, where there were public warehouses for receiving commodities, it was less than in the west, where there were none; because the people used the warehouse certificates as a medium of exchange among themselves. An inhabitant of Orange related that at this time he had accompanied his father with a load of wheat to Cross Creek, now Fayetteville, where they received 5s. a bushel for the grain, but could get only one-fifth of the price in cash. His father returned home with 40s. and was able to pay his tax, which was more than his neighbors could do.

All this was caused chiefly by a most shortsighted financial policy on the part of the provincial government. During the times of the French and Indian war the colony had made repeated issues of currency. After peace was declared in 1763 this began rapidly to be redeemed. So sudden and wide an extension of the money medium was bad in itself; but when in the face of an immense tide of immigration the currency began rapidly to contract the effect was calamitous. An idea of this may be gotten from the fact that in 1768 while the amount of money was decreasing about 10 per cent a year the population was increasing about 7 per cent a year.

The inhabitants of the back counties, isolated from, and out of sympathy with, the dominant class in the province, were thus ready material to the hand of the political agitator. Weighed down by improperly adjusted taxes, dishonest officers, excessive fees, and insufficient currency, the people only awaited the appearance of a leader under whom they might range themselves in opposition to their oppressors.

— Document No. 7 —

## SHAYSITE HOSTILITY TO LAWYERS *

*A contemporary view of Shays's Rebellion, first printed in 1788, deplores the hostility of the Shaysites to the legal profession, which resulted in 1785 in the election to the legislature of Massachusetts of a considerable number of men apparently for no other reason than that their opponents were lawyers. The second section of the reading gives a rather unflattering view of the sincerity or constancy of purpose of Daniel Shays.*

↗           ↗           ↗

The long restraints which the confusion of war had laid upon the administration of justice in private cases, occasioned a very rapid increase of civil actions, when those restraints were removed. This circumstance gave employment to the practitioners at the bar, and increased

* From George Richard Minot, *The History of the Insurrections in Massachusetts in the Year Seventeen Hundred and Eighty Six and the Rebellions Consequent Thereon* (Boston, 2nd edn., 1810), pp. 28-30, 88-89.

their numbers beyond what had been usual in the state. The profession naturally became an object of observation; and, at length, was generally spoken of as an object of reform. Advantage was taken of the prevailing jealousy against lawyers; and unfortunately, a prelude to the insurrections was framed out of it. Inflammatory writings were inserted in the newspapers, to excite an idea, in the minds of the people, that the burdens which they laboured under, were occasioned by the abuses of this profession: And, a doctrine was particularly insisted on in one of them, that this class of men ought to be abolished. The electors were therefore conjured to leave them out of publick office, and to instruct their representatives, then about to be chosen for the year 1786, to annihilate them. This idea communicated itself from very natural causes. The lawyers were odious to debtors as the legal instruments of their distresses. They were also intimately connected with the courts of justice, and in a great measure, under their control: A clamour against the one, therefore, was a kind of impeachment of the other. The transition from the servants of the courts, to the courts themselves, being easy and direct, the cry, of course, was received and spread with avidity, by those whose intentions were directed at the administration of justice in general. The flame pervaded the greatest part of the Commonwealth. The lawyers, in most instances, were excluded from the House of Representatives. Among other towns, the capital filled the seat which she had from ancient times, reserved for one of this profession, the seat where Pratt, Thacher, Otis and Adams, had drawn admiration and love from the publick eye, with a gentleman of a less unpopular calling. When the assembly met, their zeal was kindled from the people. This was first evidenced by their elections in filling up the vacancies in Senate. Preference was given to some characters, which could not be accounted for on any other grounds, than that of their fellow candidates being practitioners of the law. . . .

The continuance of the insurgent forces at Worcester, for any length of time, however desirable it might have been to their leaders, was not to be effected. Their numbers were considerable, and they had no other supplies than what a sudden departure from their several homes had allowed them to provide. . . . A large body of them with Shays their principal leader, retired [December, 1786] by the way of Rutland, at which place they remained for some time.

The retreat of these unhappy men, though less peaceable than their assembling, was attended with such distresses, as rendered them objects of pity. Some were actually frozen to death, and all of them were exposed to the inclemencies of the severest winter that had happened for many years. These difficulties were heightened by a scarcity of provisions, and, we may suppose, by an unwelcome reception among some persons, who considered them as the fomenters of sedition. Their cause during their whole expedition to Worcester, must have worn an unfavorable aspect in their own view. Indeed, this idea seemed to make a deep impression upon Shays himself, if he was sincere in a conversation which happened about this time, between him and a confidential officer of government. Shays was asked by this officer, who left it optional with him to answer the question or not, "Whether, if he had an opportunity, he would accept of a pardon, and leave his people to themselves?" To which Shays answered, "Yes, in a moment."


— Document No. 8 —

# THE CAPTURE OF JOB SHATTUCK AT GROTON*

*The retreat of Shays from Worcester was foreshadowed by the success of the state militia in the capture of his co-rebel Job Shattuck and some associates fleeing from Concord a few days earlier (November 30, 1786). The*

* From Samuel A. Green, "Groton During Shays's Rebellion," *Massachusetts Historical Society Proceedings*, 2d Series, Vol. I (1884-1885), pp. 305-306.

*following item from the* Massachusetts Gazette *of December 5, 1786, reflects in its outspoken language a strong sympathy with the point of view of the commercial interests around Boston, whose security and prosperity the Shays movement was threatening.*

↗            ↗            ↗

We have the pleasure of announcing to the publick the very agreeable and authentick information of the safe return of the corps of volunteer horse, under the command of Col. Hichborn, after having achieved the object of their expedition, by the capture of *Shattuck, Parker* and *Page,* who have been the indefatigable fomenters of sedition in the county of Middlesex.

Too much credit cannot be given the officers and men on this occasion, who performed a long and disagreeable march, a great part of the way in the night, in a heavy snow-storm, and in a very short period.—The people every where in the country, through which they passed, so far from the opposition which the rioters threatened, cheerfully gave them every assistance that was wanted. A company of horse, under Col. Wood, of Pepperell, were particularly active, and had the honour of securing two of the prisoners before the party arrived at Groton.— Shattuck, however, had found the means of eluding their vigilance—but upon the arrival of the troop in the vicinity of his house, a second search commenced with renewed ardour—until he was finally discovered, pursued and apprehended—though not without a sharp conflict with one of the horse, in which much personal bravery was displayed—but upon two others coming up, he was obliged to surrender.—Shattuck was badly wounded in the knee, and the gentleman immediately engaged received a slight cut on his face.—These deluded and daring violators of the publick peace had been in arms the day before in Concord, on their way to Cambridge, to stop the Court of Common Pleas, which is now sitting unmolested in that town.

The most absurd and contradictory stories have been circulated throughout the country; and it may be truly said, that they have supported a bad cause by the most scandalous deception, as well to their own strength, as to the views of government.

Every body joins in giving praise to the volunteers, who have done honour to their characters, and rendered the most essential benefit to the State by this achievement.

Groton is about 43 [33?] miles from this town [Boston] so that what with the direct course, and the chase which they had before the seizure of Shattuck, who immediately fled to the woods, upon being discovered behind a barn, many of the company must have rode near one hundred miles from Wednesday morning to Thursday evening, and were some of them nine hours on horse-back, without scarcely dismounting in that time. There was not a gun fired at the horse, in the whole expedition, though it was generally believed that Shattuck had forfeited his house in order to a vigorous opposition: This, however, proved not to be the case, for he had endeavoured to abscond, after trying in vain to raise a party for his protection.— The troop went in aid of the Sheriff, by order of his Excellency, when it was found that the late amnesty of government was without effect, in reclaiming these hardened offenders.

— Document No. 9 —

# COMMUNICATIONS FROM THE WHISKEY REBELS OF 1794*

*The unique method used by "Tom the Tinker" in coercing distillers into joining the resistance to the Excise Act of 1791 is shown in the following letter and advertisement in the* Gazette *of Pittsburgh. David Bradford, though prosecuting attorney of Washington County, issued the second proclamation below, calling for the mass*

* From *Pennsylvania Archives,* 2nd Series, Vol. IV (Harrisburg, 1876), pp. 71-72, 111-112.

*meeting at Parkinson's Ferry, thus emphasizing the fact that the rebellion was not one merely of embittered and embattled rustics.*

✓              ✓              ✓

MR SCULL:

I am under the necessity of requesting you to put the following in your next paper. It was found pasted to a tree, near my distillery.

JOHN REED

*July* 23, 1794.

## ADVERTISEMENT.

In taking a survey of the troops under my direction in the late expedition against that insolent exciseman, John Neville, I find there were a great many delinquents, even among those who carry on distilling. It will, therefore, be observed that I, Tom the Tinker, will not suffer any certain class or set of men to be excluded the service of this my district, when notified to attend on any expedition carried on in order to obstruct the execution of the excise law, and obtain a repeal thereof.

And I do declare on my solemn word, that if such delinquents do not come forth on the next alarm, with equipments, and give their assistance as much as in them lies, in opposing the execution and obtaining a repeal of the excise law, he or they will be deemed as enemies, and stand opposed to virtuous principles of republican liberty, and shall receive punishment according to the nature of the offense.

And whereas, a certain John Reed, now resident in Washington, and being at his place near Pittsburgh, called Reedsburgh, and having a set of stills employed at said Reedsburgh, entered on the excise docket, contrary to the will and good pleasure of his fellow citizens, and came not forth to assist in the suppression of the execution of said law, by aiding and assisting in the late expedition, have, by delinquency, manifested his approbation to the execution of the aforesaid law, is hereby charged forthwith to cause the contents of this paper, without adding or diminishing, to be published in the Pittsburgh

*Gazette,* the ensuing week, under the no less penalty than the consumption of his distillery.

Given under my hand, this 19th day of July, one thousand seven hundred and ninety-four.

TOM THE TINKER

*David Bradford to the Inhabitants of Monongahela, Virginia.*

*Washington, Aug. 6, 1794.*

GENTLEMEN:—I presume you have heard of the spirited opposition given to the excise law in this State. Matters have been so brought to pass here, that all are under the necessity of bringing their minds to a final conclusion. This has been the question amongst us some days: Shall we disapprove of the conduct of those engaged against Neville the excise officer or approve? Or in other words, shall we suffer them to fall a sacrifice to Federal prosecution, or shall we support them? On the result of this business we have fully deliberated and have determined with head, heart, hand and voice that we will support the opposition to the excise law. The crisis is now come, submission or opposition. We are determined in the opposition. We are determined in future to act agreeably to system, to form arrangements, guided by reason, prudence, fortitude and spirited conduct. We have proposed a general meeting of the four counties of Pennsylvania, and have invited our brethren in the neighboring counties in Virginia to come forward and join us in council and deliberation on this important crisis, and conclude upon measures interesting to the western counties of Pennsylvania and Virginia. A notification of this kind may be seen in the Pittsburgh paper. Parkinson's Ferry is the place proposed, as most central, and the 14th of August the time. We solicit you (by all the ties of an union of interest can suggest) to come forward to join us in our deliberations. The cause is common to us all; we invite you to come, even should you differ with us in opinion; we wish you to hear our reasons influencing our conduct.

Yours with esteem,<br>DAVID BRADFORD.

# — Document No. 10 —

# OFFICIAL REPORTS ON THE WHISKEY REBELLION*

*Governor Thomas Mifflin of Pennsylvania appointed Chief Justice Thomas M'Kean and General William Irvine as commissioners to confer with the insurgent farmer-distillers and their sympathizers. The following letters, one to Irvine from a subordinate and the other from the commissioners to the governor, tell about the concentration of disaffected militia on Braddock's Field, August 1, and the assault on revenue agent John Neville on July 16-17, 1794.*

✓　　　　　✓　　　　　✓

*John Wilkins to William Irvine.*

*Pittsburg, Aug. 19, 1794.*

DEAR SIR:

I HERE give you a true statement, as far as it came within my knowledge, of the assembling of people on Braddocks Field's on Friday, the first inst., and their march through this place on Saturday, the 2d inst.

In the beginning of that week, we were informed that the Pittsburg Mail had been taken from the Post, and in consequence of letters found therein, Expresses were riding through all the Four Counties, warning the men, to turn out with their arms, and to appear on Braddocks Field's, Friday at one o'clock, under the penalty of having their property destroyed by fire.

That day were to march from thence to Pittsburg, (or Sodom as they called the Town) and destroy it by fire, as also to take the Garrison. This news we repeatedly heard, but at length some of their particular friends, as

* From Townsend Ward, "The Insurrection of the Year 1794, in the Western Counties of Pennsylvania," *Pennsylvania Historical Society Memoirs,* Vol. VI (Philadelphia, 1858), pp. 183-185, 203.

was supposed, came into Town and gave certain intelligence, that the intention of the people was to destroy all the Town, without respect to persons or property.

In consequence of which, a Town meeting was called, to consult on what measures were to be taken on this alarming crisis. Thursday evening and the Court House were the time and place appointed. . . . Just as the people were meeting at the Court House, four gentlemen arrived in Town from Washington Co. Supposing they were come with some despatches or accounts from the people, we appointed three gentlemen to wait on them; after some time, the three returned, and informed us, that those four gentlemen from Washington Co. had been sent by the people to offer us proposals, which were, that we immediately banish Major Kirkpatrick, Mr. Bryson, Major Butler, and a certain Day, and march to Braddocks Field's in the morning, and join the army which was to assemble there; otherwise, our town must be consumed. These were the terms; the four gentlemen were not empowered to make the least alterations; they further told us, that they must make report to the people on Braddocks Field's tomorrow early in the day, as also our answer. We inquired how many might be expected to meet on the Field; they told us, that, on a moderate calculation, seven or Eight thousand; these gentlemen further told a few of us, privately, that it was with great difficulty the people were brought to offer us any terms. When Mr. Ross and a few gentlemen in and near Washington, understood the business for which the people were assembling, they proposed joining them, in order the better, to divert them from such a horrid action. They said, that after Mr. Ross joined the people, he and some more laboured among their committees night and day, until they at last got them to make this offer to the people of Pittsburg.

Thus hearing our sentence, and the conditions, we did not long deliberate, we were no match, no relief could be given from the garrison, they were busy laying in provisions, and fortifying, in order to protect themselves and the stores.

The Committee of Twenty-one . . . was immediately appointed, we waited on the gentlemen proscribed, all but Major Butler, told them our situation. Mr. Bryson and Major Kirkpatrick declared themselves happy in thinking that their departing the town, would be a means of saving it, and that they would go in the morning. Mr. Day appeared displeased and obstinate, however, he agreed also to go in the morning; the Committee then drew up their resolves you see in the papers. Mr. Scull printed all night, in order to have a sufficient number to distribute amongst the people on Braddocks Field's, hoping this, together with our other compliance to their orders, would moderate the rage of the people for that time, and save the town, for the four gentlemen also told us privately, that they much doubted all we could do would not stop the rage of the people, when assembled on the field. . . . By the time the business was finished, it was about 2 o'clock in the night. I then came home, my family were in tears; and I believe most of the Women in town were in tears: the people appeared (by the lights) to be all stirring, and I believe the most of them hiding property. I also began to hide or bury property: the County Books and Treasury, the books belonging to my office, as Justice, my private Books, and money left in my hand by other people, a little money of my own, together, with other small property, I buried that night. I concluded the House and remainder of my property would be consumed, as my son John was so threatened by the people for buying Excise Whiskey. . . . I rather suspected that if they did not burn all the town, that, at least, the property of the obnoxious people would be consumed, and as his store was in one end of my house, all would go together. In the morning the greatest confusion prevailed amongst the people, all sorts of labour and business ceased, all the men preparing to march, the women in tears, some leaving the town, some hiding property, and some so shocked as not to know what to do. . . . At nine o'clock, Major Kirkpatrick and Mr. Brison set out on their journey: I conveyed them to the river, and saw them arrive at Robinson's, our parting was distressing, to see our fellow-citizens banished, as in a moment, from their all, without a hearing, and for what we know without a just cause, was too much for any human heart to bear.

*Pittsburg*                        22d *of August,* 1794

On Monday we endeavoured to ascertain the facts that

led immediately to the riots in this county on the 16th
and 17th of last month, at General Neville's estate, and
the result is as follows: The Marshal for the district of
Pennsylvania had process to serve upon divers persons
residing in the counties of Fayette and Alleghany, and
had executed them all (above thirty) without molestation
or difficulty, excepting one, which was against a Mr.
Shaw: he or some other person went to the place were
Dr. Beard, the Brigade Inspector for Washington county,
was hearing appeals made by some of the militia of a
battalion, who had been called upon for a proportion of
the quota of this state of eighty thousand men, to be in
readiness agreeably to an act of Congress; there were
upwards of fifty there with their fire-arms, to whom it was
related, that the federal sheriff, as they styled the Marshal, had been serving writs in Alleghany county, and
carrying the people to Philadelphia for not complying
with the excise laws, and that he was at General Neville'
house. It was then in the night of the 15th of last month;
between thirty and forty flew instantly to their arms, and
marched toward Mr. Neville's, about twelve miles distant,
where they appeared early next morning. Your Excellency has already heard the tragical event. It should be
added, that the delinquents, against whom the Marshal
had process, told him that they would enter their stills,
and pay him the excise, together with the costs of suit.
Major Lenox applauded their prudent conduct, and told
them, that, though he had not authority to comply with
their wishes, yet if they would enter their stills with the
inspector, and procure his certificate, and send it to
Philadelphia, upon payment of the money due with the
costs, he was persuaded all further prosecutions would
be stayed.

If this detail is true, it is evident the outrages committed
at Mr. Neville's were not owing to deliberate precon-
certed measures, but originated in an unbridled gust of
passion artfully raised amongst young men, who may have
been at the time too much heated with strong drink!

We met accordingly, and conversed together (with the
twelve conferees appointed by the Parkinson's Ferry meeting of the 14th of August) freely for several hours. The
supposed grievances were numerous; but they dwelt
principally on their being sued in the courts of the United

States, and compelled to attend trial, at a distance of
three hundred miles from their places of abode, before
judges, and jurors, who are strangers to them, and by
whom the credit due to witnesses entirely unknown
could not be properly estimated, and the inability to pay
the excise owing to the restrained state of their trade and
commerce. Impressed with the idea, that the spirit of
the people in these counties, may be diffused into other
counties and states, we have urged the necessity of a
speedy termination of this business, and to that end, the
calling the committee of sixty together, at an earlier day
than the one fixed upon; though the gentlemen press
upon us to allow time to the people to cool, yet we
believe that they will gratify us in this request. We are
acquainted personally with the committee of twelve, and
think them well disposed.

— Document No. 11 —

# THE FEUDAL NATURE OF LANDHOLDING IN RENSSELAERWYCK *

*The anomalous position of a supposed tenant, who,
though presumably the owner of his farm because he can
sell it, yet has to forfeit a quarter of the price to the over-
lord to whom he and his ancestors have paid rents and
personal services and who has no protection against the
whims of the lord of the manor and his friends as they
destroy fences and crops on a hunting party, is revealed
in the following legislative reports.*

* From *Documents of the Assembly of the State of New
    York,* Vol. VI, No. 271 (Albany, 1840), pp. 1-3; Vol. VII,
    No. 189 (Albany, 1844), pp. 1-4.

*Report of the Committee on so much of the Governor's Message as relates to the difficulties between the landlord and tenants of the Manor of the Rensselaerwyck* [1840].

REPORTS:

That the Manor of Rensselaerwyck, as possessed and claimed by the proprietors, comprises a large tract of country, beginning at Bearen island, in the Hudson River, running thence north up the river twenty-four miles, and extending inland on each side of the river twenty-four miles. . . . The lands in the Manor are nearly all held under perpetual leases. . . . By these leases, all mines and streams of water are reserved, together with all rights necessary and proper to render the use of the same available . . . to have free ingress and egress, and liberty to lay out roads. . . . The rents reserved are payable in wheat, to be delivered at the mansionhouse of the proprietor. There is also reserved a certain proportion of the purchase or consideration money, usually one-fourth, whence the right is familiarly termed *quarter-sales*, upon every alienation of the premises. . . . It is also provided that if the rent is not paid within twenty-eight days the landlord shall have the right to distrain; and that if no sufficient distress can be found upon the premises, or any of the covenants of the lease shall be broken, . . . he may re-enter . . . and . . . the lease shall . . . become void. Most of the leases, in addition to the payment of rent in wheat, require one or more days' service with wagon and horses, and the delivery . . . of a certain number of fowls.

It appears that the continuance of the relation existing between landlord and tenant . . . is not desired by either party. The proprietor is willing to sell . . . but a wide difference exists as to the price which should be paid. The tenants conceiving themselves aggrieved, and their minds becoming inflamed by what they considered oppression . . . were led . . . to the unjustifiable course of resisting by force the execution of legal process. . . . The difficulties assumed so threatening an aspect that the Governor found himself compelled to call out a military force. . . .

The Governor . . . speaking of the tenures by which the lands in the Manor of Rensselaerwyck are held: "Such tenures introduced before the revolution are regarded as inconsistent with existing institutions, and have become odious to those who hold under them. They are unfavorable to agricultural improvement, inconsistent with the prosperity of the districts where they exist, and opposed to sound policy. . . . The extent of the territory . . . and the great numbers of our fellow citizens interested . . . render the subject worthy of the consideration of the Legislature."

*Report of the select committee, to whom was referred the petitions from numerous tenants of the manor of Rensselaerwyck* [1844].

The American people are emphatically an emigrating people. From almost every township in the older States, large colonies of farmers and mechanics have emigrated to new settlements in the west. But many of the tenants of the manor of Rensselaerwyck are unable to avail themselves, without great sacrifice, of the privilege enjoyed by their fellow citizens in other sections of the Union. If they wish to dispose of their property, one quarter of its price is liable to be forfeited to the proprietor. . . . A restriction of this nature . . . must be regarded as extremely unjust and oppressive . . . operating most effectually to check if not to arrest altogether the prosperity of that community. . . . In many countries of Europe, this, as well as other barbarous features of the feudal system, have long since been abolished.

It is a source of just pride with the American farmer, that he is the proprietor of the soil which he cultivates. This honorable feeling cannot be shared by the unfortunate tenant. . . . He cultivates the soil of another, and is liable at any time, to have his growing crops destroyed, or his fences demolished by the proprietors of the manor, in the exercise of some one of the numerous privileges reserved to them in their leases. He is consequently depressed by these influences, which tend to generate in the American farmer of more favored districts that spirit of independence which is not humbled by the payment of an annual tribute, acknowledges no superior, and which raises him to a rank in the social scale, never attained by the working man of any country but our own.

# — Document No. 12 —

# ORIGINS OF FREE-HOMESTEAD AGITATION*

*The homestead doctrine evolved by George Henry Evans, a New York labor editor, and his associates between 1835 and 1844, was a toned-down adaptation from Thomas Skidmore's agrarianism. Evans would end all disposal of public lands for any other purpose than free homesteads for the easing of poverty and labor tensions in the eastern labor centers. His proposals as set forth in his* Working Man's Advocate *in 1844, recognizing the further need of government assistance in getting the laborers to the land and giving them a start, might, if Congress had fully complied, have made of the Homestead Act of 1862 a workable instrument.*

✓   ✓   ✓

### EQUAL RIGHTS TO LAND
[March 16, 1844]

The leading measure that we shall propose in this paper is *the Equal Right* of every man to the free use of a sufficient portion of the Earth to till for his *subsistence*. If man has a right to LIVE, as all subsistence comes from the earth, he has a right, in a state of nature, to a portion of its spontaneous products; in a state of civilization, to a portion of the earth to till for his subsistence. This right is now, no matter why, in possession of a comparative

* From *The Working Man's Advocate* (New York), March 16, 1844.

few, many of whom possess not only a sufficiency, but a superfluity, of land: yet we propose not to divest them of that superfluity, against their consent. We simply propose that the inequality extend no further; that *Government* shall no longer traffic or permit traffic in that which is the property of no man or government; that the Land shall be left, as Nature dictates, free to the use of those who choose to bestow their labor upon it.

We propose that the Public Lands of the States and of the United States shall be *free to actual settlers,* and to actual settlers only; that townships of six miles square shall be laid out in Farms and Lots, of any vacant one of which a man, *not possessed of other land,* may take possession and keep same during his life or pleasure, and with the right to sell his *improvements,* at any time, to any one *not possessed of other land.* . . .

We shall be told, perhaps, as we have been told occasionally by persons who had not reflected on the subject, that the public lands are so cheap *now* as to be accessible to all industrious persons who desire to settle on them. It is not so. Though the nominal price of the lands is one dollar and twenty-five cents an acre, the real price to the actual settler is nearer *ten dollars* an acre, unless he chooses to become a squatter and trust to Congress for the privilege of purchasing his land at the government price; for the speculator, under the present system, goes ahead of the settler, picks out the best and most eligibly situated tracts, pays for them with paper money (itself a *monstrous cheat*) or its profits, and when the actual settler comes, he must either pay the speculator's price or go further into the wilderness, where he must struggle for years under the disadvantage of conveying his surplus products over bad roads to a distant market.

But suppose that the settler could obtain lands near a market at the government price, they would still be as inaccessible to the *bulk* of our surplus laboring population as if they were in the hands of the speculators. Some few become settlers under the present system; a few more might become so if speculation in land was entirely prohibited; but it needs that the lands should be *free,* in order that the surplus laborers may be absorbed; for the expense of removal to the lands, and of the necessary stock and provisions to bring them into successful

cultivation, is more than many could meet. Many of the
employed laborers, however, who might be able to meet
these expenses, would gladly exchange their life of ser-
vitude for one of independence, even at the risk of
encountering some hardships; and these would leave
vacancies that might be filled by those unable to emigrate. . . .

If we were to take a census of New York for the purpose, we should probably find ten thousand men who
desire or are preparing to emigrate to the Public Lands.
Our proposition is equivalent to giving all such the sum of
*two hundred dollars each,* for they would have to pay that
amount for one hundred and sixty acres. . . .

Two hundred dollars, then at the least, and probably
much more, will be saved by every emigrant to the Public
Lands, from New York or elsewhere, if the plan that we
have proposed is adopted by the people.

— Document No. 13 —

# CONGRESSIONAL OPINIONS ON FREE HOMESTEADS*

*About everything that could be said for and against
the homestead bill was uttered in the House of Representatives in 1852 (a decade before the passage of any
act). The two samples, from Orlando B. Ficklin of Illinois, for, and Volney E. Howard of Texas, against the
bill, agree on the greatest weakness, which finally made
the law relatively ineffective.*

✓          ✓          ✓

* From *Congressional Globe,* 32 Cong., 1 Sess., Appendix,
pp. 523, 583-584.

*Orlando B. Ficklin of Illinois*          *April* 24, 1852

We are told by some that they are apprehensive, if this bill should pass, that there will be a rush from the old States to the new States—a kind of general stampede in the direction of the western and north and southwestern portions of this country. That will not be the case, however. In the first place, there are a great many individuals who are attached to home, kindred, and the fireside of their youth. This is a strong feeling of the human heart, and one, too, which is not so readily relinquished. This feeling alone will prevent many from quitting the home of their childhood. Those who are able to purchase will not select a tract of land in this new wilderness country, but will prefer to buy a home of their choice, land that has been improved by the erection of comfortable houses, and other conveniences, rather than take one not of their choice, and remain on it five years before perfecting their title.

There is still another class that will not avail themselves of this bill; they are such as are too poor to find means to pay the expense of emigrating from the older to the new States, and of settling on these lands; therefore those persons cannot go. When, then, you come to make the calculation, you will find that those not now residents of the new States, who will secure to themselves the benefits of this bill, will be generally of the middle, or rather not of the very poorest class, and that the number will not be so large by a great deal as is anticipated by some gentlemen. The man who is too poor to purchase land, but who has means to defray traveling expenses, will go and select him a home under this bill, improve the land and obtain a patent for it at the end of five years; but the man who is too poor to reach the lands cannot, of course, enjoy their benefits.

*Volney E. Howard of Texas*          *April* 21, 1852

But, sir, I deny the constitutional power of Congress to grant away the public property in donations to the poor. This Government is not a national almshouse. We have no right to collect money by taxation, and then divide the proceeds among the people generally, or those who are destitute of land, food, or raiment. . . . There is no sound distinction between giving money by direct appropriations from the Treasury, and land, in the purchase of which that money has been invested. It is no more the property of the nation in one case than in the other, nor less an appropriation. What right have we to tax the property and industry of all classes of society to purchase homesteads, and enrich those who may not be the possessors of the soil? . . .

It is a great mistake to suppose that you will materially better the condition of the man in the old States, or the Atlantic cities, by giving him one hundred and sixty acres of land in the far West. The difficulty with him is not that of procuring the land, but to emigrate himself and family to the country where it is, and to obtain the means of cultivating it. Without this the grant is useless to the poor man. The gift, to make it efficient, should be followed up by a further donation to enable the beneficiary to stock and cultivate it. It would be a far greater boon to all our citizens, of native and foreign origin, to furnish them for a few dollars, a rapid means of reaching the land States in the West; and this, in my opinion, may be accomplished by exercising the legitimate powers of the Government, and without drawing upon the Treasury, or diminishing the value of the public domain as a source of revenue.

— Document No. 14 —

# THE FARMERS' DECLARATION OF INDEPENDENCE*

*The embattled farmers of 1870-1900 had a strong sense of historical precedent. They sometimes couched their complaints or set forth their programs in the form of paraphrases of revered documents of the past, and held*

* From the *Prairie Farmer*, Vol. XLIV, July 12, 1873, p. 217.

*their conclaves on holidays celebrating the nation's glory.
Thus the Populists had their Washington's Birthday and
Fourth of July conventions in 1892. But the Grangers
preceded them by nearly a decade in a "Farmers' Declaration of Independence" in the panic year of 1873.*

✓          ✓          ✓

When in the course of human events, it becomes necessary for a class of people, suffering from long continued
systems of oppression and abuse, to rouse themselves from
an apathetic indifference to their own interests, which has
become habitual; to assume among their fellow citizens,
that equal station, and demand from the government they
support, those equal rights to which the laws of nature,
and of nature's God entitles them; a decent respect for
the opinions of mankind requires that they should declare
the causes that impel them to a course so necessary to
their own protection.

We hold these truths to be self-evident: That all men
are created equal; that they are endowed by their creator
with certain inalienable rights; that among these are life,
liberty, and the pursuit of happiness. That to secure these
rights governments are instituted among men, deriving
their just powers from the consent of the governed; that
whenever the powers of a government become destructive
of these, either through the injustice or inefficiency of its
laws or through the corruption of its administrators, it is
the right of the people to abolish such laws, and institute
such reforms as to them shall seem most likely to effect
their safety and happiness. Prudence indeed will dictate
that laws long established shall not be changed for light
and trifling causes, and accordingly, all experience hath
shown that mankind are more disposed to suffer while
evils are sufferable, than to right themselves by abolishing
the laws to which they are accustomed. But when a long
train of abuses and usurpations, pursuing invariably the
same object, evinces a desire to reduce a people under
the absolute despotism of combinations, that, under the
fostering care of government, and with wealth wrung
from the people, have grown to such gigantic proportions
as to overshadow all the land, and wield an almost ir-
resistible influence for their own selfish purposes, in all its
halls of legislation, it is their right—it is their duty to

throw off such tyranny, and provide new guards for their future security.

Such has been the patient sufferance of the producing classes of these states, and such is now the necessity which compels them to declare that they will use every means save a resort to arms to overthrow this despotism of monopoly, and to reduce all men claiming the protection of American laws to an equality before those laws, making the owner of a railroad as amenable thereto as the "veriest beggar that walks the streets, the sun and air his sole inheritance."

The history of the present railway monopoly is a history of repeated injuries and oppressions, all having in direct object the establishment of an absolute tyranny over the people of these states unequalled in any monarchy of the Old World, and having its only parallel in the history of the Medieval ages, when the strong hand was the only law, and the highways of commerce were taxed by the Feudal Barons, who from their strongholds, surrounded by their armies of vassals, could levy such tribute upon the traveler as their own wills alone should dictate. To prove this let facts be submitted to a candid world:

They have influenced our executive officers, to refuse their assent to laws the most wholesome and necessary for the public good, and when such laws have been passed they have utterly refused to obey them.

They have procured the passage of other laws, for their own benefit alone, by which they have put untold millions into their own coffers, to the injury of the entire commercial and industrial interests of the country.

They have influenced legislation to suit themselves, by bribing venal legislators to betray the true interests of their constituents, while others have been kept quiet by the compliment of free passes.

They have repeatedly prevented the re-election of representatives, for opposing with manly firmness, their invasion of the people's rights.

They have by false representations and subterfuge induced the people to subscribe funds to build roads, whose rates, when built, are so exorbitant, that in many instances transportation by private conveyance is less burdensome.

They have procured charters by which they condemn

and appropriate our lands without adequate compensation therefor, and arrogantly claim that by virtue of these charters they are absolutely above the control of legal enactments.

They have procured a law of congress by which they have dispossessed hundreds of farmers of the homes that by years of toil they have built up; have induced others to mortgage their farms for roads never intended to be built, and after squandering the money thus obtained, have left their victims to the mercy of courts over which they have held absolute sway.

They have obstructed the administration of justice by injunctions procured from venal judges, by legal quibbles and appeals from court to court, with intent to wear out or ruin the prosecutor, openly avowing their determination to make it so terrible for the public to prosecute them that they will not dare undertake it.

They have virtually made judges dependent on their will alone, and have procured their appointment for the express purpose of reversing a decision of the highest court of the nation, by which millions were gained to them, to the injury of the holders of the bonds and the breaking down of this last safeguard of American freemen.

They have affected to render themselves independent of and superior to the civil power, by ordering large bodies of hirelings to enforce their unlawful exactions, and have protected them from punishment for an injury they might inflict upon peaceful citizens, while ejecting them from their conveyances for refusing to pay more than the rate of fare prescribed by laws.

They have arrested and summoned from their homes for trial, at distant points, other citizens for the same offense of refusing to pay more than the legal fare, putting them to as great inconvenience and expense as possible, and still further evincing their determination to make it too terrible for the people to dare engage in any legal conflict with them.

They have combined together to destroy competition and to practice an unjust discrimination, contrary to the expressed provisions of our constitution and the spirit of our law.

They have virtually cut off our trade with distant parts

of the world by their unjust discriminations and by their exorbitant rates of freights, forcing upon us the alternative of accumulating upon our hands a worthless surplus, or of giving three-fourths of the price our customers pay for their products for their transportation.

Under the false and specious pretense of developing the country, they have obtained enormous grants of public lands from congress, and now retard rather than develop its settlement, by the high prices charged for such land.

They have converted the bonds fraudulently obtained from the government, into a great corruption fund, with which they are enabled to bribe and control legislatures, and subvert every branch of government to their own base and sordid purpose.

They have increased the already intolerable burden of taxation, which the people have to endure, compared with which the tea and stamp tax which precipitated the war of the revolution, seems utterly insignificant, by the appropriation of money from the public treasury, while they have escaped taxation themselves by evading and violating the expressed provisions of their charters.

In every stage of these oppressions we have petitioned our legislatures for redress in the most humble terms. Our repeated petitions have been answered only by silence, or by attempts to frame laws that shall seem to meet our wants, but that are, in fact, only a legal snare for courts to disagree upon and for corporations to disobey.

Nor have we been wanting in attempts to obtain redress through congress. We have warned them from time to time of these various and repeated encroachments upon our rights; we have reminded them of the circumstances of our emigration and settlement here; we have appealed to them as the administrators of a free and impartial government, to protect us from these encroachments, which, if continued, would inevitably end in the utter destruction of those liberties for which our fathers gave their lives, and the reinstatement of privileged classes and an aristocracy of wealth, worse than that from which the war of the revolution freed us. They too have been deaf to the voice of justice and of duty. We must therefore acquiesce in the necessity which compels us to denounce their criminal indifference to our wrongs, and hold them as we hold our legislators—enemies to the producer—to the monopolists, friends.

We, therefore, the producers of this state in our several counties assembled, on this the anniversary of that day that gave birth to a nation of freemen and to a government of which, despite the corruption of its officers, we are still so justly proud, appealing to the Supreme Judge of the world for the rectitude of our intentions, do solemnly declare that we will use all lawful and peaceable means to free ourselves from the tyranny of monopoly, and that we will never cease our efforts for reform until every department of our government gives token that the reign of licentious extravagance is over, and something of the purity, honesty and frugality with which our fathers inaugurated it has taken its place.

That to this end we hereby declare ourselves absolutely free and independent of all past political connections, and that we will give our suffrage only to such men for office, from the lowest officer in the state to the president of the United States, as we have good reason to believe will use their best endeavors to the promotion of these ends; and for the support of this declaration, with a firm reliance on Divine Providence, we mutually pledge to each other our lives, our fortunes, and our sacred honor.

— Document No. 15 —

# SILVER LEGISLATION OF 1873, 1878, AND 1890*

*The demonetization of the standard silver dollar in 1873 caused legislative wrangling for the rest of the century. The Bland-Allison Act of 1878 and the Sherman*

* From *U. S. Statutes at Large,* Vol. XVII, pp. 424-436; *ibid.,* Vol. XX, pp. 25-26; *ibid.,* Vol. XXVI, pp. 289-290.

*Act of 1890 were palliatives satisfactory to neither the free-silver nor the gold-standard advocates. Then on October 30, 1893, Congress repealed the purchase clause of the Sherman Act, thus restoring virtually the situation of twenty years earlier. Thereafter, the single gold standard, defined by law in 1900, remained undisturbed until 1933. Portions of the laws immaterial to the relation between gold and silver are omitted from the following excerpts.*

✓ ✓ ✓

## THE "CRIME OF 1873"

SEC. 13. That the standard for both gold and silver coins of the United States shall be such that of one thousand parts by weight nine hundred shall be of pure metal and one hundred of alloy. . . .

SEC. 14. That the gold coins of the United States shall be a one-dollar piece, which, at the standard weight of twenty-five and eight-tenths grains, shall be the unit of value; a quarter-eagle, or two-and-a-half dollar piece, a three-dollar piece; a half-eagle, or five-dollar piece; an eagle, or ten-dollar piece; and a double eagle, or twenty-dollar piece. . . .

SEC. 15. That the silver coins of the United States shall be a trade dollar, a half-dollar, or fifty-cent piece, a quarter-dollar, or twenty-five cent piece, a dime, or ten-cent piece; and the weight of the trade-dollar shall be four hundred and twenty grains troy; the weight of the half-dollar shall be twelve grams (grammes) and one-half of a gram, (gramme;) the quarter-dollar and the dime shall be respectively, one-half and one-fifth the weight of said half-dollar; and said coins shall be a legal tender at their nominal value for any amount not exceeding five dollars in any one payment. . . .

SEC. 17. That no coins, either of gold, silver, or minor coinage, shall hereafter be issued from the mint other than those of the denominations, standards and weights herein set forth. . . .

SEC. 21. That any owner of silver bullion may deposit the same at any mint, to be formed into bars, or into dollars of the weight of four hundred and twenty grains, troy, designated in this act as trade-dollars, and no deposit of silver for other coinage shall be received. . . .

SEC. 25. That the charge for converting standard gold bullion into coin shall be one-fifth of one per centum; and the charges for converting standard silver into trade-dollars . . . shall be fixed, from time to time, by the director, but with the concurrence of the Secretary of the Treasury, so as to equal but not exceed, in their judgment, the actual average cost to each mint and assay-office of the material, labor, wastage, and use of machinery employed in each of the cases aforementioned. . . .

SEC. 67. That this act shall be known as the "Coinage act of eighteen hundred and seventy-three;" and all other acts and parts of acts pertaining to the mints, assay-offices, and coinage of the United States inconsistent with the provisions of this act are hereby repealed. . . .

APPROVED, *February 12*, 1873.

## THE BLAND-ALLISON ACT OF 1878

*An act to authorize the coinage of the standard silver dollar, and to restore its legal-tender character*

BE IT ENACTED BY THE SENATE AND HOUSE OF REPRESENTATIVES OF THE UNITED STATES OF AMERICA IN CONGRESS ASSEMBLED, That there shall be coined, at the several mints of the United States, silver dollars of the weight of four hundred and twelve and a half grains Troy of standard silver, as provided in the act of January eighteenth, eighteen hundred thirty-seven, on which shall be the devices and superscriptions provided by said act; which coins together with all silver dollars heretofore coined by the United States, of like weight and fineness, shall be a legal tender, at their nominal value, for all debts and dues public and private, except where otherwise expressly stipulated in the contract. And the Secretary of the Treasury is authorized and directed to purchase, from time to time, silver bullion, at the market price thereof, not less than two million dollars worth per month, nor more than four million dollars worth per month, and cause the same to be coined monthly, as fast as so purchased, into such dollars; and a sum sufficient to carry out the foregoing provision of this act is hereby ap-

propriated out of any money in the Treasury not otherwise appropriated. And any gain or seigniorage arising
from this coinage shall be accounted for and paid into
the Treasury, as provided under existing laws relative to
the subsidiary coinage: *Provided,* That the amount of
money at any one time invested in such silver bullion,
exclusive of such resulting coin, shall not exceed five
million dollars: *And provided further,* That nothing in
this act shall be construed to authorize the payment in
silver of certificates of deposit issued under the provisions
of section two hundred and fifty-four of the Revised
Statutes. . . .

SEC. 3. That any holder of the coin authorized by this
act may deposit the same with the Treasurer or any
assistant treasurer of the United States, in sums not less
than ten dollars, and receive therefor certificates of not
less than ten dollars each, corresponding with the denominations of the United States notes. The coin deposited
for or representing the certificates shall be retained in
the Treasury for the payment of the same on demand.
Said certificates shall be receivable for customs, taxes, and
all public dues, and when so received, may be reissued.

SEC. 4. All acts and parts of acts inconsistent with the
provisions of this act are hereby repealed.

[Passed over the President's veto, February 28, 1878.]

## THE SHERMAN SILVER PURCHASE ACT
### OF 1890

. . . The Secretary of the Treasury is hereby directed
to purchase, from time to time, silver bullion to the aggregate amount of four million five hundred thousand
ounces, or so much thereof as may be offered in each
month, at the market price thereof, not exceeding one
dollar for three hundred and seventy-one and twenty-five
hundredths grains of pure silver, and to issue in payment
for such purchases of silver bullion Treasury notes of the
United States to be prepared by the Secretary of the
Treasury, in such form and of such denominations, not
less than one dollar nor more than one thousand dollars,
as he may prescribe, and a sum sufficient to carry into
effect the provisions of this act is hereby appropriated
out of any money in the Treasury not otherwise appropriated.

SEC. 2. That the Treasury notes issued in accordance with the provisions of this act shall be redeemable on demand, in coin, at the Treasury of the United States, or at the office of any assistant treasurer of the United States, and when so redeemed may be reissued; but no greater or less amount of such notes shall be outstanding at any time than the cost of the silver bullion and the standard silver dollars coined therefrom, then held in the Treasury purchased by such notes; and such Treasury notes shall be a legal tender in payment of all debts, public and private, except where otherwise expressly stipulated in the contract, and shall be receivable for customs, taxes, and all public dues, and when so received may be reissued; and such notes, when held by any national banking association, may be counted as a part of its lawful reserve. That upon demand of the holder of any of the Treasury notes herein provided for the Secretary of the Treasury shall, under such regulations as he may prescribe, redeem such notes in gold or silver coin, at his discretion, it being the established policy of the United States to maintain the two metals on a parity with each other upon the present legal ratio, or such ratio as may be provided by law.

SEC. 3. That the Secretary of the Treasury shall each month coin two million ounces of the silver bullion purchased under the provisions of this act into standard silver dollars until the first day of July eighteen hundred and ninety-one, and after that time he shall coin of the silver bullion purchased under the provisions of this act as much as may be necessary to provide for the redemption of the Treasury notes herein provided for, and any gain or seigniorage arising from such coinage shall be accounted for and paid into the Treasury. . . .

SEC. 5. That so much of the act of February twenty-eighth, eighteen hundred and seventy-eight, entitled "An act to authorize the coinage of the standard silver dollar and to restore its legal-tender character," as requires the monthly purchase and coinage of the same into silver dollars of not less than two million dollars, nor more than four million dollars' worth of silver bullion, is hereby repealed. . . .

Approved, July 14, 1890.

# THE POPULIST SUBTREASURY PLAN*

*The following plan, as devised by C. E. Macune of the Southern Alliance, appeared in the national newspaper of the organization late in 1889. An elaborate bill with all the administrative features filled in, but omitting barley, rye, rice, sugar and wool from the list of products covered, was ready for submission to Congress in 1891. Congress ignored the proposal, which then became an essential feature of the Populist platform.*

✔          ✔          ✔

. . . For this purpose let us demand that the United States government modify its present financial system:

1.  So as to allow the free and unlimited coinage of silver or the issue of silver certificates against an unlimited deposit of bullion.

2. That the system of using certain banks as United States depositaries be abolished, and in the place of said system, establish in every county in each of the States that offers for sale during the one year five hundred thousand dollars worth of farm products: including wheat, corn, oats, barley, rye, rice, tobacco, cotton, wool, and sugar, all together; a sub-treasury office, which shall have in connection with it such warehouses or elevators as are necessary for carefully storing and preserving such agricultural products as are offered it for storage, and it should be the duty of such sub-treasury department to receive such agricultural products as are offered for storage and make a careful examination of such products and class same as to quality and give a certificate of the deposit showing the amount and quality, and that United States legal-tender paper money equal to eighty per cent of the local current value of the products has been advanced on same on interest at the rate of one per cent per

* From *The National Economist* (Washington), December 21, 1889, p. 216.

annum, on the condition that the owner or such other person as he may authorize will redeem the agricultural product within twelve months from date of the certificate or the trustee will sell same at public auction to the highest bidder for the purpose of satisfying the debt. Besides the one per cent interest the sub-treasurer should be allowed to charge a trifle for handling and storage, and a reasonable amount for insurance, but the premises necessary for conducting this business should be secured by the various counties donating to the general government the land and the government building the very best modern buildings, fireproof and substantial. With this method in vogue the farmer, when his produce was harvested, would place it in storage where it would be perfectly safe and he would secure four-fifths of its value to supply his pressing necessity for money at one per cent per annum. He would negotiate and sell his warehouse or elevator certificates whenever the current price suited him, receiving from the person to whom he sold, only the difference between the price agreed upon and the amount already paid by the sub-treasurer. When, however, these storage certificates reached the hand of the miller or factory, or other consumer, he to get the product would have to return to the sub-treasurer the sum of money advanced, together with the interest on same and the storage and insurance charges on the product.

— Document No. 17 —

# FARMERS ALLIANCE PLATFORMS OF 1889*

*The Northwestern Alliance and the Southern Alliance held simultaneous but separate conventions in St. Louis*

* From Frank M. Drew, "The Present Farmers' Movement," *Political Science Quarterly,* Vol. VI (June, 1891), pp. 293-294, for the Northwestern platform; *The National Economist,* December 21, 1889, pp. 214-215, for the Southern.

*in December, 1889. Each drew up its own set of resolutions, the two being quite similar in some respects, but containing seemingly irreconcilable differences. A comparison of the two platforms may make somewhat understandable why union could be effected only by the formation of a new third party.*

↗　　　　↗　　　　↗

*Northwestern Alliance Platform*　　　December 6, 1889

WHEREAS, the farmers of the United States are most in number of any order of citizens, and with other productive classes have freely given of their blood to found and maintain the nation; therefore be it

RESOLVED, that the public land, the heritage of the people, be reserved for actual settlers only, and that measures be taken to prevent aliens from acquiring titles to lands in the United States and Territories, and that the law be rigidly enforced against all railroad corporations which have not complied with the terms of their contract, by which they have received large grants of land.

2. We demand the abolition of the national banking system and that the government issue full legal tender money direct to the people in sufficient volume for the requirements of business.

3. We favor the payment of the public debt as rapidly as possible, and we earnestly protest against maintaining any bonds in existence as the basis for the issue of money.

4. We favor a graded income tax, and we also favor a tax on realestate mortgages.

5. We demand economy and retrenchment as far as is consistent with the interests of the people in every department of the government, and we will look with special disfavor upon any increase of the official salaries of our representatives or government employees.

6. We favor such a revision and reduction of the tariff that the taxes may rest as lightly as possible upon productive labor and that its burdens may be upon the luxuries and in a manner that will prevent the accumulation of a United States Treasury surplus.

7. The stability of our government depends upon the moral, manual and intellectual training of the young, and we believe in so amending our public school system that the education of our children may inculcate the es-

sential dignity necessary to be a practical help to them in after life.

8. Our railroads should be owned and managed by the government, and be run in the interest of the people upon an actual cash basis.

9. That the government take steps to secure the payment of the debt of the Union and Central Pacific railroads and their branches by foreclosure and sale, and any attempt to extend the time again for the payment of the same beyond the present limit will meet with our most emphatic condemnation.

10. We are in favor of the early completion of a ship canal connecting the great lakes with the Gulf of Mexico, and a deep water harbor on the southern coast in view of opening trade relations with the Central and South American states, and we are in favor of national aid to a judicious system of experiments to determine the practicability of irrigation.

11. We sympathize with the just demands of labor of every grade and recognize that many of the evils from which the farming community suffers oppress universal labor, and that therefore producers should unite in a demand for the reform of unjust systems and the repeal of laws that bear unequally upon the people.

12. We favor the Australian system, or some similar system of voting, and ask the enactment of laws regulating the nomination of candidates for public office.

13. We are in favor of the diversification of our productive resources.

14. We [will] favor and assist to office such candidates only as are thoroughly identified with our principles and who will insist on such legislation as shall make them effective.

## Southern Alliance Platform          December 6, 1889

Agreement made this day by and between the undersigned committee representing the National Farmers Alliance and Industrial Union on the one part, and the undersigned committee representing the Knights of Labor on the other part, Witnesseth: The undersigned committee representing the Knights of Labor, having read the demands of the National Farmers Alliance and Industrial Union which are embodied in this agreement, hereby endorse the same on behalf of the Knights of Labor, and for the purpose of giving practical effect to the demands herein set forth, the legislative committees of both organizations will act in concert before Congress for the purpose of securing the enactment of laws in harmony with the demands mutually agreed.

And it is further agreed, in order to carry out these objects, we will support for office only such men as can be depended upon to enact these principles into statute law uninfluenced by party caucus.

The demands hereinbefore referred to are as follows:

1. That we demand the abolition of national banks and the substitution of legal tender treasury notes in lieu of national bank notes, issued in sufficient volume to do the business of the country on a cash system; regulating the amount needed on a per capita basis as the business interests of the country expand; and that all money issued by the Government shall be legal tender in payment of all debts public and private.

2. That we demand that Congress shall pass such laws as shall effectually prevent the dealing in futures of all agricultural and mechanical productions; preserving a stringent system of procedure in trials as shall secure the prompt conviction, and imposing such penalties as shall secure the most perfect compliance with the law.

3. That we demand the free and unlimited coinage of silver.

4. That we demand the passage of laws prohibiting the alien ownership of land, and that Congress take early steps to devise some plan to obtain all lands now owned by aliens and foreign syndicates; and that all lands now held by railroad and other corporations in excess of such as is actually used and needed by them, be reclaimed by the Government and held for actual settlers only.

5. Believing in the doctrine of "equal rights to all and special privileges to none," we demand that taxation, National or State, shall not be used to build up one interest or class at the expense of another.

We believe that the money of the country should be kept as much as possible in the hands of the people, and hence we demand that all revenues, National, State or county, shall be limited to the necessary expenses of the

Government economically and honestly administered.

6. That Congress issue a sufficient amount of fractional paper currency to facilitate exchange through the medium of the United States mail.

7. We demand that the means of communication and transportation shall be owned and operated in the interest of the people as is the United States postal system.

For the better protection of the interests of the two organizations, it is mutually agreed that such seals or emblems as the National Farmers Alliance and Industrial Union of America may adopt, will be recognized and protected in transit or otherwise by the Knights of Labor, and that all seals and labels of the Knights of Labor will in like manner be recognized by the members of the National Farmers Alliance and Industrial Union of America.

— Document No. 18 —

# PRELIMINARIES TO THE ORGANIZATION OF THE POPULIST PARTY*

*The Southern Alliance took the lead in a convention at Ocala, Florida, in December of 1890, and restated its policies, but again failed to achieve unity of the various agricultural and labor organizations. Further conventions at Omaha in February, 1891, and at Cincinnati in the following May paved the way for the unity convention at St. Louis and the full organization of the Populist party at Omaha in 1892. The following platforms and resolu-*

* From *The National Economist*, December 20, 1890, p. 216;
*ibid.*, February 7, 1891, p. 333; *ibid.*, May 30, 1891, p. 162.

*tions of 1890 and 1891, though quite repetitious, reveal
the development of the ultimate Populist demands.*

✓                    ✓                    ✓

*Ocala Convention, December 2, 1890.*
*Report of the Committee on Demands*

1. *a.* We demand the abolition of national banks.

*b.* We demand that the government shall establish
sub-treasuries or depositories in the several States, which
shall loan money direct to the people at a low rate of
interest, not to exceed two per cent per annum, on non-
perishable farm products, and also upon real estate, with
proper limitations upon the quantity of land and amount
of money.

*c.* We demand that the amount of the circulating
medium be speedily increased to not less than $50 per
capita. . . .

2. That we demand that Congress shall pass such laws
as shall effectually prevent the dealing in futures of all
agricultural and mechanical productions; preserving a
stringent system of procedure in trials as shall secure the
prompt conviction, and imposing such penalties as shall
secure the most perfect compliance with the law.

3. We condemn the silver bill recently passed by Congress, and demand in lieu thereof the free and unlimited
coinage of silver.

4. We demand the passage of laws prohibiting alien
ownership of land, and that Congress take prompt action
to devise some plan to obtain all lands now owned by
aliens and foreign syndicates; and that all lands now held
by railroads and other corporations in excess of such as is
actually used and needed by them be reclaimed by the
government, and held for actual settlers only.

5. Believing in the doctrine of "equal rights to all and
special privileges to none," we demand that our national
legislation shall be so framed in the future as not to build
up one industry at the expense of another; and we further
demand a removal of the existing heavy tariff tax from
the necessities of life that the poor of our land must have;
we further demand a just and equitable system of graduated tax on incomes; we believe that the money of the
country should be kept as much as possible in the hands

of the people, and hence we demand that all national and State revenues shall be limited to the necessary expenses of the government economically and honestly administered.

6. We demand the most rigid, honest, and just State and national governmental control and supervision of the means of public communication and transportation, and if this control and supervision does not remove the abuse now existing, we demand the government ownership of such means of communication and transportation.

7. We demand that Congress of the United States submit an amendment to the constitution providing for the election of United States Senators by direct vote of the people of each state.

*Omaha Convention, 1891.*

That we most emphatically declare against the present system of government as manipulated by the Congress of the United States and the members of the legislatures of the several States; therefore,

We declare in favor of holding a convention on February 22, 1892, to fix a date and place for the holding of a convention to nominate candidates for the office of President and Vice-President of the United States.

We declare that in the convention to be held on February 22, 1892, . . . representation shall be one delegate from each State in the Union.

That we favor the abolition of national banks, and that the surplus funds be loaned to individuals upon land security at a low rate of interest.

That we demand the foreclosure of mortgages that the government holds on railroads.

That the President and Vice-President of the United States should be elected by popular vote, instead of by an electorial college.

That the Alliance shall take no part as partisans in a political struggle by affiliating with Republicans or Democrats.

That we favor the free and unlimited coinage of silver.

That the volume of currency be increased to $50 per capita.

That all paper money be placed on an equality with gold.

That we as land-owners pledge ourselves to demand

that the Government allow us to borrow money from the United States at the same rate of interest as do the banks.

That Senators of the United States shall be elected by vote of the people.

*Cincinnati Convention, May 19-20, 1891.*

[*Platform in full.*]

1. That in view of the great social, industrial, and economical revolution now dawning on the civilized world and the new and living issues confronting the American people, we believe that the time has arrived for a crystalization of the political reform forces of our country and the formation of what should be known as the People's party of the United States of America.

2. That we most heartily indorse the demands of the platforms as adopted at St. Louis, Mo., in 1889; Ocala, Fla., in 1890, and Omaha, Neb., in 1891, by industrial organizations there represented, summarized as follows:

*a.* The right to make and issue money is a soverein power to be maintained by the people for the common benefit. Hence we demand the abolition of national banks as banks of issue, and as a substitute for national bank notes we demand that legal tender Treasury notes be issued in sufficient volume to transact the business of the country on a cash basis without damage or especial advantage to any class or calling, such notes to be legal tender in payment of all debts, public and private, and such notes, when demanded by the people, shall be loaned to them at not more than 2 per cent per annum upon non-perishable products, as indicated in the sub-treasury plan, and also upon real estate, with proper limitation upon the quantity of land and the amount of money.

*b.* We demand free and unlimited coinage of silver.

*c.* We demand the passage of laws prohibiting alien ownership of land, and that Congress take prompt action to devise some plan to obtain all lands now owned by alien and foreign syndicates, and that all land held by railroads and other corporations in excess of such as is actually used and needed by them be reclaimed by the government, and held for actual settlers only.

*d.* Believing the doctrine of equal rights of all and special privileges to none, we demand that taxation, national, state, or municipal, shall not be used to build up one interest or class at the expense of another.

*e.* We demand that all revenue—national, state, or county—shall be limited to the necessary expenses of the government, economically and honestly administered.

*f.* We demand a just and equitable system of graduated tax on income.

*g.* We demand the most rigid, honest and just national control and supervision of the means of public communication and transportation, and if this control and supervision does not remove the abuses now existing we demand the government ownership of such means of communication and transportation.

*h.* We demand the election of President, vice-President, and United States Senators by a direct vote of the people.

3. That we urge united action of all progressive organizations in attending the conference called for February 22, 1892, by six of the leading reform organizations.

4. That a national central committee be appointed by this conference to be composed of a chairman, to be elected by this body, and of three members from each state represented, to be named by each state delegation.

5. That this central committee shall represent this body, attend the national conference on February 22, 1892, and, if possible, unite with that and all other reform organizations there assembled. If no satisfactory arrangement can be effected, this committee shall call a national convention not later than June 1, 1892, for the purpose of nominating candidates for President and vice-President.

6. That the members of the central committee for each state where there is no independent political organization, conduct an active system of political agitation in their respective states.

Resolved, That the question of universal suffrage be recommended to the favorable consideration of the various states and territories.

Resolved, That while the party in power in 1879 pledged the faith of the nation to pay a debt in coin that had been contracted on a depreciated currency, thus adding nearly $1,000,000,000 to the burdens of the people, which meant gold for the bondholders and depreciated currency for the soldier, and holding that the men who imperiled their lives to save the life of a nation should have been paid in money as good as that paid to the bond-holders—we demand the issue of legal tender treasury notes in sufficient amount to make the pay of the soldiers equal to par with coin, or such other legislation as shall do equal and exact justice to the Union soldiers of this country.

Resolved, That as eight hours constitute a legal day's work for government employes in mechanical departments, we believe this principle should be further extended so as to apply to all corporations employing labor in the different states of the Union.

Resolved, That this conference condemns in unmeasured terms the action of the directors of the World's Columbian Exposition on May 19, in refusing the minimum rate of wages asked for by the labor organizations of Chicago.

Resolved, That the Attorney General of the United States should make immediate provision to submit the act of March 2, 1889, providing for the opening of Oklahoma to homestead settlement, to the United States Supreme Court, so that the expensive and dilatory litigation now pending there be ended.

— Document No. 19 —

# THE FORMATION OF THE POPULIST PARTY*

*In the conferences and conventions of 1889-1891, there had been a considerable amount of wavering back and forth, as one faction or another had been in the majority, over a number of issues. Take, for example, regulation or*

* From *The National Economist,* March 5, 1892, p. 396; *ibid.,* July 9, 1892, pp. 257-258.

*ownership of the railroads and, if ownership, the super-*
*fluous matter of recovering land grants and government*
*loans. A close scrutiny of the offerings of the February*
*22 and July 4 conventions in 1892 will reveal to what*
*extent the factions achieved unity and consistency of*
*purpose.*

✓              ✓              ✓

*St. Louis, [February 22], 1892*

## PLATFORM

### FINANCE

First—We demand a national currency, safe, sound
and flexible, issued by the general government only, a full
legal tender for all debts, public and private; and that
without the use of banking corporations a just, equitable
and efficient means of distribution direct to the people at
a tax not to exceed 2 per cent be provided, as set forth
in the sub-treasury plan of the Farmers Alliance, or some
better system; also, by payments in discharge of its obligations for public improvements.

*a.* We demand free and unlimited coinage of silver.

*b.* We demand that the amount of circulating medium
be speedily increased to not less than $50 per capita.

*c.* We demand a graduated income tax.

*d.* We believe that the money of the country should be
kept as much as possible in the hands of the people, and
hence we demand all national and State revenue shall be
limited to the necessary expenses of the government economically and honestly administered.

*e.* We demand that postal savings banks be established
by the government for the safe deposit of the earnings of
the people and to facilitate exchange.

### LAND

Second—The land, including all the natural resources
of wealth, is the heritage of all the people and should not
be monopolized for speculative purposes, and alien
ownership of land should be prohibited. All land now held
by railroads and other corporation in excess of their actual
needs, and all lands now owned by aliens, should be re-

claimed by the government and held for actual settlers only.

## TRANSPORTATION

Third—Transportation being a means of exchange and a public necessity, the government should own and operate the railroads in the interest of the people.

*a.* The telegraph and telephone, like the post-office system, being a necessity for transmission of news, should be owned and operated by the government in the interest of the people. . . .

Resolved, That the question of female suffrage be referred to the legislatures of the different States for favorable consideration.

Resolved, That the government should issue legal tender notes and pay the Union soldier the difference between the price of the depreciated money in which he was paid and gold.

Resolved, That we hail this conference as the consummation of a perfect union of hearts and hands of all sections of our common country. The men who wore the gray and the men who wore the blue meet here to extinguish the last smoldering embers of civil war in the tears of joy of a united and happy people, and we agree to carry the stars and stripes forward forever to the highest point of national greatness.

*Omaha Convention of* [*July 4,*] 1892.

### UNION OF THE PEOPLE

First. That the union of the labor forces of the United States this day consummated shall be permanent and perpetual; may its spirit enter into all hearts for the salvation of the republic and the uplifting of mankind.

Second. Wealth belongs to him who creates it, and every dollar taken from industry without an equivalent is robbery. "If any will not work, neither shall he eat." The interests of rural and civic labor are the same; their enemies are identical.

Third. We believe that the time has come when the railroad corporation will either own the people or the people must own the railroads; and, should the government enter upon the work of owning and managing all railroads, we should favor an amendment to the Constitution by which all persons engaged in the government service shall be placed under a civil service regulation of the most rigid character, so as to prevent the increase of the power of the national administration by the use of such additional government employes.

## THE QUESTION OF FINANCE

We demand a national currency, safe, sound, and flexible, issued by the general government only, a full legal tender for all debts, public and private, and that without the use of banking corporations, a just, equitable, and efficient means of distribution direct to the people at a tax not to exceed 2 per cent per annum, to be provided as set forth in the sub-treasury plan of the Farmers Alliance, or a better system; also by payments in discharge of its obligations for public improvements.

We demand free and unlimited coinage of silver and gold at the present legal ratio of 16 to 1.

We demand that the amount of circulating medium be speedily increased to not less than $50 per capita.

We demand a graduated income tax.

We believe that the money of the country should be kept as much as possible in the hands of the people, and hence we demand that all State and national revenues shall be limited to the necessary expenses of the government, economically and honestly administered.

We demand that postal savings banks be established by the government for the safe deposit of the earnings of the people and to facilitate exchange.

## CONTROL OF TRANSPORTATION

Transportation being a means of exchange and a public necessity, the government should own and operate the railroads in the interest of the people.

The telegraph and telephone, like the post-office system being a necessity for the transmission of news, should be owned and operated by the government in the interest of the people.

## RECLAIMING THE LAND

The land, including all the natural sources of wealth, is the heritage of the people, and should not be monopolized for speculative purposes, and alien ownership of land should be prohibited. All land now held by railroads and other corporations in excess of their actual needs and all lands now owned by aliens should be reclaimed by the government, and held for actual settlers only.

[Intercalation by *The National Economist*] The following resolutions were offered independent of the platform, and were adopted, as expressive of the sentiment of the convention:

Resolved, That we demand a free ballot and a fair count in all elections, and pledge ourselves to secure it to every legal voter without Federal intervention through the adoption by the States of the unperverted Australian secret ballot system.

Resolved, That the revenue derived from a graduated income tax should be applied to the reduction of the burden of taxation now levied upon the domestic industries of this country.

Resolved, That we pledge our support to fair and liberal pensions to ex-Union soldiers and sailors.

Resolved, That we condemn the fallacy of protecting American labor under the present system, which opens our ports to the pauper and criminal classes of the world and crowds out our wage earners, and we denounce the present ineffective law against contract labor, and demand the further restriction of undesirable emigration.

Resolved, That we cordially sympathize with the efforts of organized workingmen to shorten the hours of labor, and demand a rigid enforcement of the existing eight-hour law on government work, and ask that a penalty clause be added to the said law.

Resolved, That we regard the maintenance of a large standing army of mercenaries, known as the Pinkerton system, as a menace to our liberties, and we demand its abolition, and we condemn the recent invasion of the Territory of Wyoming by the hired assassins of plutocracy, assisted by Federal officers.

Resolved, That we commend to the thoughtful consideration of the people and the reform press the legislative system known as the initiative and referendum.

Resolved, That we favor a constitutional provision limiting the office of President and Vice-President to one term, and providing for the election of the Senators by a direct vote of the people.

Resolved, That we oppose any subsidy or national aid to any private corporation for any purpose.

# — Document No. 20 —

# THE KENTUCKY NIGHT RIDERS*

*In 1907 and 1908, there were numerous items and articles in the newspapers and magazines about the violent activities of the burley-tobacco growers of Kentucky in their struggle to break the price-fixing practices of the American Tobacco Company. Though deploring the use of force, some of the writers showed strong sympathy for the farmers who were threatened by starvation as a consequence of absurdly low prices. The following parts of two articles give a more complete picture than either of them separately.*

[*Harper's Weekly*]

There is war in Kentucky. In a score of towns what is virtually a state of martial law exists. In the farming districts cellars have been fortified and loaded arms stacked within easy reach. The "Night Riders" are abroad. . . . The rebellion had its origin two years ago. Certain of the planters awoke to a realization of what they alleged to be the "grip of the trust." Forthwith they began to preach the doctrine of "a trust against a trust."

* From Charles V. Tevis, "A Ku-Klux Klan of Today," *Harper's Weekly,* Vol. LII (February 8, 1908), pp. 14-16, 32; Martha McCulloch-Williams, "The Tobacco War in Kentucky," *American Review of Reviews,* Vol. XXXVII (February, 1908), pp. 168-170.

They vowed that they had no hand in the making of prices for their tobacco; that in order to live, pay their debts, and continue the raising of tobacco they had to accept what was offered them, and that the interest on their investment of labor and money was not worthwhile. Hundreds of farmers flocked to this standard; five associations, unions in effect, were formed and affiliated under one name, the "American Society of Equity"; and the cry for higher prices was loudly raised.

In the course of months, 75,000 members were enrolled in the two big societies, the Burley Tobacco Association and the Dark Tobacco Association. This membership represented a tobacco pool of 350,000,000 pounds, or more than seventy per cent of the State's output. . . . But the leaders of the movement appreciated the fact that for it to be successful there must be no non-unionists, and a greater crusade was instituted. As has been said, persuasions failed to bring all of the independent growers into the fold. Then came the Night Riders.

This was the beginning of a crusade of destruction which has up to this time caused the loss of $50,000,000 worth of property and the sacrifice of several lives. As yet nothing has served to check it.

Not one, but a half-dozen companies, of from 200 to 500 men each . . . are parading nightly, blackened ruins marking their progress.

On the night of the second of March, 1906, they appeared suddenly in the streets of Princeton. They were on horseback, masked, armed, determined. With a preliminary scattering of shots, they applied the torch to several freight cars containing tobacco, some of which had been bought by the American Tobacco Company, and the rest owned by independents. Not until these fires had completely destroyed the tobacco did they leave the city and disappear into the darkness as mysteriously as they had come. . . .

Close upon the heels of this event came a report that a band of mounted men, masked and armed, had burned the barns of a farmer near Hopkinsville. Simultaneously, other planters—all independents—communicated the intelligence that their crops had been "salted," or ruined by "dragging," or that their barns had been burned. These arrived from different parts of the State, and each stated that a band of mounted men, masked and armed, had committed the depredations. . . .

Then appeared the ominous skull and cross-bones on the front doors, fences, and barns of independents, who were refusing to join in the fight against the tobacco trust. Letters threatening destruction of property and a whipping were sent out broadcast. A campaign of intimidation was waged, and the American Society of Equity's ranks were augmented. But the American Tobacco Company and its allied concerns pursued the even tenor of their way, strong in the support of those who laughed at threats and remained independent.

This was not well advised. On the night of December 7 began a reign of terror that has no like in the history of Kentucky. Hopkinsville was the point of first attack. The citizens of this city . . . little suspected what the next few hours held for them. . . . Not until their slumbers were broken by the clatter of flying hoofs and the rattle of shots, and their sleep-burdened eyes blinded by the glare of burning buildings, did they realize the full meaning of a descent by the dreaded band.

In the face of a determined fire from the several detachments of the invaders, the men of the city . . . ventured from the protection of their homes to meet in alleys and in the shadows of buildings. . . . [The defenders] at length joined for a concerted attack upon the marauders, who were holding the public square. There a pitched battle ensued.

The spectacle . . . was painted red by the flames of the blazing warehouses. . . . Slowly, fighting each step of retreat, the "Night Riders" were forced from street to street and alley to alley, and finally to the outskirts of the city. There two of the raiders were seen to fall from their horses as the bullets flew among them. The army of citizens had by this time assumed formidable size, but in the face of its terrific fire the invaders made a last stand. . . . Then, with a threat to repeat the outrage, the band galloped away. . . .

[In] the third big raid of the "Night Riders," . . . at Russellville, . . . several citizens were seriously wounded, and $100,000 worth of property was destroyed.

The band entered the city shortly after midnight without a moment's warning. A detachment overpowered the

police officials, binding them hand and foot. Another detachment went to the Louisville and Nashville railroad
yards, where they took possession of every locomotive,
fearing that whistles would be sounded and the alarm
given to the countryside. The electric-light plant was
also seized, and its whistles spiked. Others of the band
tied telegraph operators to doors and, at the point of
revolvers, held up the telephone operators, . . . at the
same time wrecking the apparatus. . . .

The main body of the raiders proceeded directly to the
work of incendiarism. Within a brief time flames from
the factory of the American Snuff Company and the warehouses of Luckatt and Wade were reddening the heavens.
The warehouses of the Standard Oil Company, a planing
mill, a wagon factory, a grocery, a livery stable, and a
private residence within the fire zone were soon ablaze.
After leaving their usual bloody trade mark, by shooting
down three citizens who incautiously ventured upon the
streets, the "Night Riders" left the scene.

The following night the masked host rode in Campbell
County, across the Ohio River from Cincinnati. On
Monday, January 6, the Riders appeared almost simultaneously at the towns of Bethel, Sherburne, and Jackstown. The first, a village, was practically wiped off the map;
all the American Tobacco Company's property at Sherburne was burned to the ground; and only a timely warning and a quick removal of the independent's tobacco at
Jackstown saved that community. . . .

The destruction . . . has . . . but whetted the determination of the masked raiders to accomplish by dreadful
might what peaceful conferences failed in doing.

[*Scenes from the* Review of Reviews]

An ordinary screen-door . . . is the last thing from
which one would expect a curdly thrill in this year of
peace. Save in one particular this door was nowise unlike
a million others, in other homesteads,—it swung true on
its hinges and had wire of a fine mesh. But amid the
meshes, and on the frame, there were the marks of
forty-seven bullets. The bullets had been fired upon an
August night of 1907, when only the screen door protected the family sleeping inside. The bullets came quar-
tering,—five hundred of them it may be, maybe even a

thousand. Some bored round holes through window-panes, others penetrated weatherboarding, laths, and plaster, and sped on to bury themselves in the opposite wall. Still others zipped along the roof, chipping shingles in their flight. They were revolver bullets, or those from Winchester rifles. So many were there, and fired at such close range, it is almost a miracle that any soul within reach of them escaped alive.

Five people were within reach of them,—Stephen Moseley, a farmer of Trigg County, Ky., his wife, and his three sons. Mr. Moseley was wounded in three places; his wife came near losing an eye through having fragments of screen-wire driven into it. The lads saved themselves by dropping from their beds to the floor, at their mother's order, and rolling as far out of range as was possible. The telephone wire had been cut before the attack. There were possibly 100 men in the attacking party. After the shooting they called Moseley out, whipped him hard, warned him not to seek legal redress, then rode away, whooping and yelling. . . . The cause was the tobacco fight, the occasion a suspicion of disloyalty on his part toward the Planters' Protective Association, the organization of tobacco growers that is waging the fight. . . . Moseley had been laggard in joining the embattled farmers. . . .

The association was born of imperious necessity. Tobacco prices had fallen, fallen until they were much below the cost of production. . . . Tobacco requires throughout hard hand labor, and plenty of it. It is ready for market the fall and winter after growth. Current rates for tobacco in January, 1904, meant, according to Kentucky calculations, less than 30 cents a day for an able-bodied man's work in raising it. Out of the 30 cents he must feed, clothe, and lodge himself and his family. . . . The association is in essence a selling trust, opposed to the buying monopolies. It takes in hand the tobacco pledged to it, fixes the price, and holds until something gives way, somewhere. . . . Absolute control of this tobacco supply spells victory for the organization. The hill billy is what stands in the way of this absolute control. . . . The night rider discourages him in ways better befitting Russia than free America. Scraping plant-beds, thus destroying all chance of a crop, is one of them, almost the mildest; burning sacked wheat, newly threshed, or haystacks, or barns, another. Blowing up threshing machines whose owners dare thresh for hill billys is still another. Add whippings, threats, scrawled coffins and cross-bones, the pulling up of young tobacco, the killing of pasturing stock, yet still the tale of outrages is incomplete. These things, no less than the shooting up of farmsteads, are directed at individuals. The night-riding mass, when fairly and fully in stride, goes out to shoot up and burn out a town. . . .

Against all this let it be clearly set forth that the association has accomplished certain results. By raising the price of tobacco from less than $4 per 100 pounds to a fraction more than $9 it has brought the plain people up out of the miry pit, the slough of debt and despond, and set their feet in the way of prosperity.

## — Document No. 21 —

# OFFICIAL REPORT ON CONDITIONS IN THE GRAIN TRADE*

*The wheat growers of North Dakota and their Nonpartisan League were guilty of no demagoguery when they placed a considerable part of the blame for their lack of prosperity upon the tricks and ruses of the grain dealers. The following extracts from the summary of a report made in 1922 by the Federal Trade Commission indicates how accurate were most of the major charges made by the insurgent farmers and their political spokesmen.*

* From Federal Trade Commission, *Terminal Grain Marketing* (Vol. III of *The Grain Trade,* Washington, 1922), pp. 9-12.

The public or private terminal elevator companies operating as grain dealers are the largest merchandisers and distributors in the trade. Several of the larger elevator companies combine with merchandising and warehousing a cash and future commission business and the operation of country elevators.

The chief profit of terminal elevator merchandisers is of course derived from the purchase and sale of grain. The indications are, particularly at Chicago, that a substantial proportion of this profit is often realized by the mixing of different grades of grain to raise the commercial value.

In addition to the foregoing sources of profit terminal elevator companies operating as merchandisers derive a considerable revenue from various auxiliary operations, such as the sale of screenings obtained from cleaning operations, transactions in the futures market, and from the storage, transfer, cleaning, and conditioning of grain for others in return for a fee. . . .

Practically every private terminal elevator company engaged in merchandising makes a practice of mixing, cleaning, and conditioning, either to secure screenings, to improve the quality of the grain, or to take advantage of the latitude within the requirements of each standard grade by mixing to the bottom level of such requirements. Different grades are frequently mixed also in railroad operated elevators under the supervision of local inspection departments with a view to releasing additional bin space. Combined results of wheat-mixing operations in Chicago in six private elevators for a four-year period gave an outturn of 93.6 per cent No. 2 winter as compared with 42.6 per cent received, and an outturn of 90 per cent No. 1 spring wheat as against 38.9 per cent received. . . . A comparison of the mixing results for terminal elevators in Chicago, Minneapolis, Duluth, and Kansas City on all contract grades (No. 1 and No. 2 of both spring and winter wheat) specified by rule on each exchange for four years was as follows: At Chicago, 45.7 per cent in, 95 per cent out; at Minneapolis, 31.4 per cent in, 34.4 per cent out; at Duluth, 36.9 per cent in, 72.4 per cent out; at Kansas City, 36.1 per cent in, 51.6 per cent out. An attempt to determine statistically the probable profits per bushel from mixing operations at

Minneapolis and Duluth for five years gave a range of from about one-fourth to 3 1/3 cents per bushel at Minneapolis and from about two-thirds of a cent to about 4 1/2 cents per bushel at Duluth. . . .

From what has just been said, it would seem that grain merchandising on the part of operators of licensed public elevators is contrary to sound principles of public warehousing. The possible remedy for this situation suggested by the circumstances is to make it practicable for grain dealers not operating elevators to store grain in public elevators in competition with the big elevator merchandisers. To accomplish this would require a reduction in storage charges. But the indications are that, even at present storage rates, a purely storage and transfer elevator can not be profitably operated at interior terminal points.

The problem in question can be met in either one of two ways. The railroads might be required to operate elevators for the convenience of their shippers; or the Government, presumably the State government, might operate storage elevators at rates sufficiently low to permit dealers without elevators to compete with the elevator merchandisers. . . .

All the incidents of terminal handling should be arranged so as to eliminate incentives to unduly prompt selling and premature removal from storage at the terminal elevator of the railroad on which the grain originates, and so as to facilitate the continued ownership of the grain by the country shipper, if his judgment of economic conditions suggest such a policy. Possibly the initial elevation and storage charge should uniformly be included in the freight charge, so that only through-billed grain would escape contributing something toward the cost of storage facilities at the railroad elevator. Such a measure would tend to prevent holding grain in cars and the tying up of railroad equipment, as well as the diversion of grain to private elevators for speculative purposes.

The restoration of a more normal situation as regards the use of public storage in the grain trade would be so generally beneficial to the trade and to the public as to warrant necessary legal reforms and financial expenditures in the directions suggested, or whatever other steps might be necessary to accomplish the object in view.

— Document No. 22 —

# THE NONPARTISAN LEAGUE'S ANSWER TO THE GRAIN TRADE*

*The recommendation of the Federal Trade Commission (in the preceding document) for public-owned elevators to compete with private ones, and especially the final suggestion for legal reforms to any extent necessary, sounds like a federal blessing on the action by the legislature of North Dakota in 1919. All of the essential reform acts of the legislature in that year are in the pamphlet cited in the footnote below.*

✔        ✔        ✔

## LAW CREATING THE MILL AND ELEVATOR ASSOCIATION

SECTION 1. That for the purpose of encouraging and promoting agriculture, commerce and industry, the State of North Dakota shall engage in the business of manufacturing and marketing farm products and for that purpose shall establish a system of warehouses, elevators, flour mills, factories, plants, machinery and equipments, owned, controlled and operated by and under the name of North Dakota Mill and Elevator Association, hereinafter for convenience called the Association.

SECTION 2. The Industrial Commission shall operate, manage and control the Association, locate and maintain its places of business, of which the principal place shall be within the state, and shall make and enforce orders, rules, regulations and by-laws for the transaction of its

* From Industrial Commission of North Dakota, *Constitution, Laws and Amendments Thereto Authorizing the North Dakota Industrial Program* (Bismarck, June 1, 1921), pp. 25-27.

business. The business of the Association, in addition to other matters herein specified, may include anything that any private individual or corporation may lawfully do in conducting a similar business except as herein restricted. The Industrial Commission shall meet within twenty days after the passage and approval of this Act to begin the organization of the Association.

SECTION 3. To accomplish the purposes of this act the Industrial Commission shall acquire by purchase, lease, or by exercise of the right of eminent domain, . . . all necessary property or property rights, and may construct, remodel or repair all necessary buildings; and may purchase, lease, construct, or otherwise acquire, warehouses, elevators, flour mills, factories, offices, plants, machinery, equipments, and all other things necessary, incidental or convenient in the manufacturing and marketing of all kinds of raw and finished farm products within or without the state and may dispose of the same; and may buy, manufacture, store, mortgage, pledge, sell, exchange or otherwise acquire or dispose of all kinds of manufactured and raw farm and food products and by-products, and may for such purposes establish and operate exchanges, bureaus, markets and agencies, within or without the state, including foreign countries, on such terms and conditions, and under such rules and regulation as the Commission may determine.

SECTION 4. The Industrial Commission shall obtain such assistance as in its judgment may be necessary for the establishment, maintenance and operation of the Association. To that end it shall appoint a Manager, and may appoint such subordinate officers and employes as it may judge expedient. It may constitute such Manager its general agent, in respect to the functions of the Association, but subject, nevertheless in such agency, to the supervision, limitation and control of the commission. It shall employ such contractors, architects, builders, attorneys, clerks, accountants and other experts, agents and servants as in the judgment of the Commission the interests of the state may require, and shall define the duties, designate the titles, and fix the compensation and bonds of all such persons so engaged; provided, however, that subject to the control and regulation of the Commission, the Manager of the Association shall appoint and employ such deputies and other subordinates, and such contractors, architects, builders, attorneys, clerks, accountants and other experts, agents and servants as he shall, in his judgment, deem are required by the interests of the Association. The total compensation of such appointees and employes, together with other expenditures for the operation and maintenance of the Association, shall remain within the appropriation and earnings lawfully available in each year for such purpose. All officers and employes of the Association engaged upon its financial functions shall, before entering upon their duties, respectively furnish good and sufficient bonds to the state in such amount and upon such conditions as the Commission may require and approve; but the bond of the Manager shall not be less than fifty thousand dollars. Such bonds shall be filed with the Secretary of State.

SECTION 5. The Industrial Commission may remove and discharge any and all persons appointed in the exercise of the powers granted by this Act, whether by the Commission or by the Manager of the Association and any such removal may be made whenever in the judgment of the Commission the public interests require it; provided, however, that all appointments and removals contemplated by this Act shall be so made as the Commission shall deem most fit to promote the efficiency of the public service.

SECTION 6. The Industrial Commission shall fix the buying price of all things bought, and the selling price of all things sold, incidental to the operation of the Association, and shall fix all charges, any and all services rendered by the Association, but in fixing these prices— while all services are to be rendered, as near as may be, at cost—there shall be taken into consideration, in addition to other necessary costs, a reasonable charge for depreciation of all property, all overhead expenses and a reasonable surplus, together with all amounts required for the re-payment, with interest, of funds received from the state.

SECTION 7. —All business of the Association may be conducted under the name of "North Dakota Mill and Elevator Association." Title to property pertaining to the operation of the Association shall be obtained and conveyed in the name of "The State of North Dakota, doing business as the North Dakota Mill and Elevator Association." Written instruments shall be executed in the name of the State of North Dakota, signed by any two members of the Industrial Commission, of whom the Governor shall be one, or the Manager of the Association within the scope of his authority so to do as defined by the Industrial Commission.

SECTION 8. Civil actions may be brought against the State of North Dakota on account of causes of action claimed to have arisen out of transactions connected with the operation of the Association, upon condition that the provisions of this section are complied with. In such actions the State shall be designated as "The State of North Dakota, doing business as North Dakota Mill and Elevator Association," and the service of process therein shall be made upon the Manager of the Association. Such actions may be brought in the same manner and shall be subject to the same provisions of law as other civil actions brought pursuant to the provisions of the Code of Civil Procedure. Such actions shall be brought, however, in the county where the Association shall have its principal place of business [Exceptions]. . . .

SECTION 9. There is hereby appropriated, to carry out the purposes of this act, all moneys raised by the mill tax for terminal elevators as provided in . . . the Compiled Laws of 1913. Said moneys shall be paid to the manager of said association, and he shall place the said moneys in the general funds of the Association. Said money, together with any funds that shall be procured by the Industrial Commission through the sale of state bonds, as may be provided by law for that purpose, shall be designated as the capital of the Association.

SECTION 10. The State Examiner shall personally or through deputy examiners visit the Association at least twice annually, and shall inspect and verify the assets in its possession and under its control, with sufficient thoroughness of investigation to ascertain with reasonable certainty whether the valuations are correctly carried on its books. He shall report the results of each such examination and investigation to the Industrial Commission as soon as practicable, and to the Legislative Assembly at its next ensuing session.

SECTION 11. This Act is hereby declared to be an

emergency measure and shall take effect and be in force from and after its passage and approval.

Approved February 25, 1919.

— Document No. 23 —

# THE CEDAR COUNTY (IOWA) COW WAR*

*Resistance in southeastern Iowa to the enforcement of the law for the tuberculin inoculation of dairy cattle was a prelude to the Farmers' Holiday movement inspired by Milo Reno. Starting in Cedar County, the movement spread mainly southward and reached its climax in September, 1931. Hard times and the futility of the farm legislation of the Hoover administration, as much as suspicion of the effectiveness of inoculation and resentment against the inadequate compensation for slain "guilty" cattle, lay at the bottom of the resistance.*

✓          ✓          ✓

Tipton, Ia., Sept. 21.—Farmers objecting to compulsory tuberculosis testing of cattle today repulsed a posse of 65 officers and forced them to cease attempts to test cattle on the Jacob Lenker farm, 14 miles south of here.

William Dallas, Cedar county attorney, said he did not have a complete list of men who composed the throng of farmers today, but that one was in preparation. He said he was ascertaining against which ones an injunction previously had been issued and that legal action might result.

Learning that the officers, recruited from sheriff's staffs

* From *Chicago Daily Tribune*, September 22, 23, 1931; *The New York Times*, September 23, October 13, 1931.

in surrounding counties, were mobilizing in Tipton, the farmers gathered together a band of 200 and followed the posse to the Lenker farm, where tests were to be attempted.

Lenker has been one of the consistent objectors to the test, provided for under a law by the Iowa general assembly in 1929.

When the posse stopped its automobiles in the Lenker farmyard, the farmers surrounded the cars and dared the officers and veterinarians to emerge.

"Here's mud in your eye," was the comment of one farmer as he tossed a handful of mud at one car. Others followed suit and several windows in the automobiles were broken by rocks thrown instead of mud.

One officer got out of his automobile and was immediately pushed into the mud. Newspaper men who attempted to get pictures of the disturbance were forced from the farmyard.

A horse brought along to round up the Lenker cattle and bring them to the barn for testing was left in the truck in which it had been brought from Tipton, and the posse finally abandoned its plan and returned to this city.

The fight of the objectors against the tuberculin test has flared intermittently since the middle of last March. On Aug. 5 Judge F. O. Ellison issued an injunction restraining the farmers from interfering with the tests. On Aug. 21 the veterinarians were repulsed in attempts to test cattle at the farms of Arthur Fogg, William Butterbrodt, and William R. Hogan.

They were cited for contempt, and Fogg pleaded guilty and was fined $50. The others pleaded not guilty and were released on $800 bonds.

Tipton, Iowa, Sept. 22.—This city became an armed camp late today when the first units of National Guard troops arrived to enforce the State cattle tuberculin test law against the embattled farmers of Cedar County.

The militia was ordered out last night when sixty-five State officials went to the J. W. Lenker farm to protect the State veterinarians in their work, but were repulsed by a group of 200 farmers armed with clubs and pitch-

forks. Several of the veterinarians suffered bruises about
the face and the tires of several of their cars were cut or
pierced by pitchforks.

Some 2000 troops arrived in special trains today and
pitched camp on the Cedar County Fair Grounds. Adjt.
Gen. W. H. Bailey said martial law would be declared in
the county as soon as the troop movement had been
completed.

All day long groups of farmers straggled into town.
This evening several hundred were gathered in the streets.
They were quiet for the most part, but several declared
intention to resist the cattle test law to the limit.

A large delegation of sympathizers from Lee, Des
Moines and Keokuk Counties, it was reported, has arrived
to assist the Cedar County men should they decide to
battle the troops.

Norman Baker of Muscatine, radical Republican, who
has supported the objectors to the test, is said to have met
with Mr. Lenker and Paul Moore, leaders of the revolt,
and several hundred followers early this morning in a
secret meeting to discuss their next move.

J. C. France, the attorney who represented the Cedar
County farmers last April when they brought suit for an
injunction to suspend operation of the cattle test law, said
he thought the objectors would offer no resistance to the
troops.

On the other hand, Joseph Newell, special agent for
the Illinois Bankers' Association, who has been active in
attempts to enforce the cattle test, said the farmers were
in an ugly mood and would not allow the test without
resistance.

The show-down is expected Thursday, when the veterinarians will resume attempts to test cattle on various
Cedar County farms.

Meanwhile Governor Dan Turner, who yesterday authorized the use of troops to deal with the objectors, was
preparing to hurry here from Washington, D. C., where
he has been in the interest of farm relief.

The establishment of martial law in Cedar County will
bring to a head opposition to compulsory bovine tuberculosis test that has been evident since 1929 when the law
was passed. The law provides for testing of cattle by the

injection method. This method and compulsory testing
had both been employed in Iowa for years prior to 1929,
but only on a county-wide basis.

The farmers in . . . Southeast Iowa . . . are banded
together in an association whose purpose is to prevent the
testing. Their objection is based on the argument that the
injection system causes abortion in their herds and that it
fails to identify the cattle worst infected and does brand
as infected healthy cattle.

Des Moines, Ia., Sept. 22.—[*Repetition from the foregoing.*]

Some of the argument against the tests is to the effect
that the test is designed by unscrupulous politicians and
money interests to confiscate the property of small
farmers.

The method of indemnifying farmers whose cattle are
declared infected with tuberculosis is as follows:

The animal's worth is appraised by the owner and
veterinarian.

The carcass of the animal may be sold for meat at some
establishment under the inspection of a government inspector.

The amount of "salvage" allowed on the animal goes
to the owner.

The remainder of the appraised value of the animal is
divided into thirds. The federal government pays one-
third to the farmer and the state pays the farmer a like
sum. Thus the farmer must bear the loss of one-third of
the appraised value of the animal, minus the amount he
has received for salvage.

If a condemned cow is appraised at $150 and the
salvage amounts to $25, the federal and state govern-
ments each will pay the farmer $41.66, and the farmer
will have received for his condemned cow $108.32.

New London, Iowa, Oct., 12.—Hostility of Southeastern Iowa farmers to the State compulsory bovine
tuberculin test law again became open rebellion today as
veterinarians sought to begin inoculating Henry County
cattle.

About 500 embittered men marched on the New
London jail and freed Ronald Hart, 20, arrested for scoff-

ing at Iowa National Guardsmen engaged in dispersing 150 farmers who had gathered to hinder the testers on the farm of one of their leaders.

The arrest of the young man followed that of Mike Hennessey and Henry Connor, who likewise were among the group which heckled the military escort near the McKinnon farm. Hennessey and Connor were taken to Mount Pleasant, Henry County seat, under guard, while Hart was placed in the New London jail.

As the soldiers were attempting to disperse the crowd near the McKinnon place some of the protesters returned here. With more than 400 farmers from other counties, they overran the fire station forming the front part of the Municipal Building and broke the jail lock and cell bars to free the young man.

The throng took with them for a short distance the New London marshal, Earl Brewer, but released him unharmed.

The soldiers arrived quickly at the Municipal Building, but many of the farmers already had disappeared and the militia directed its efforts to scattering groups of farmers and onlookers. They said Hart was not being sought.

The veterinarians today were approaching the McKinnon farm when their escort of soldiers was stopped by 150 protesters. A detail of twenty troopers, followed by a machine-gun squad and 250 more soldiers, marched upon the angry farmers.

The latter refused to disperse, however, and Brig. Gen. Park A. Findley, commanding the Mount Pleasant Camp, ordered the detail to move upon the crowd with drawn bayonets.

Connor cried out:

"Hang me, shoot me, arrest me. I'm just a farmer here, standing on my rights. I am not trying to resist."

He was arrested and the crowd was subdued. They permitted the McKinnon herd of thirty-five cattle to be tested, and seemingly the rebellion was crushed.

— Document No. 24 —

# INCIDENTS IN THE FARM HOLIDAY MOVEMENT*

*The imposing of what was virtually martial law in Henry County, Iowa, in 1931, including the jailing of a farmer for ostentatious nonresistance and of a boy for jeering at the militia, must have been remembered by Reno and his Farmers' Holiday associates eleven months later during their milk strike around Sioux City. Disrespect for the sheriffs' posses and for the militia finally led to violence and extreme indignity visited upon a county judge.*

Sioux City, Iowa, Aug. 13 [1932].—The strike of milk producers in Sioux City territory for higher prices resulted today in disturbances during which hundreds of gallons of milk were poured out on nearly every highway entering the city.

The most serious disturbance was on the highway between Elk Point, S. D., and Sioux City. At the town of Jefferson, trucks loaded with milk were deluged with water from the city mains and forced to turn back. At Elk Point they obtained deputy sheriffs to escort them, after the Sheriff had ordered the city authorities of Jefferson to turn off the water supply.

At the Big Sioux River Bridge more than 300 dairy farmers, on strike to keep milk from entering the city, attempted to block the trucks, but the drivers, instructed by the South Dakota officers, drove onto the bridge at high speed.

The strikers scattered, but followed across the bridge in their own automobiles and attempted to force the trucks

* From *The New York Times,* August 14, 16, 1932; *ibid.,* April 28, 1933.

to the curb. Sioux City policemen were forced to display pistols to prevent wrecking of the trucks.

On highways near Lemars, Cherokee, Merrill, Movile, Sloan, Iowa, and near Homer, Hubbard and Jackson, Neb., milk was dumped or the drivers of trucks were forced to return to their dairies with their loads of milk.

Milk producers made good their promise to supply Sioux City people with milk free of charge by establishing a depot, where persons calling with buckets, bottles and jugs received two quarts free. More than 500 gallons were dispensed in this manner, it is said.

Milk producers in the city say that while their supplies from old producers in the surrounding territory have fallen off, there is no shortage and there will be no shortage because they are bringing in milk from Omaha and elsewhere by train.

The strikers have been receiving $1 per 100 pounds, testing 3.5 per cent butter fat. They are demanding $2.17. Milk in the city is retailing at 8 cents a quart.

Des Moines, Iowa, Aug. 15.—A farmers' strike, begun a week ago in seemingly mild protest against low prices for farm products, tonight had effected a tightening blockade of the Sioux City terminal as its leaders considered extending the movement to other States.

Picketing, boycott and threats were invoked by the farmers in Northwest Iowa to advance the strike, which would withhold produce from markets until producers are assured that production costs plus a fair profit will be realized.

Stockyards in Sioux City, one of the major livestock markets of the country, today received 3,500 animals as compared to 6,500 a week ago and 8,500 on the corresponding date last year.

Hundreds of farm men and women barricaded roads to prevent produce-laden trucks from entering Sioux City, and a crisis there was considered close at hand.

Produce dealers in Kingsley, a small town a few miles from Sioux City, were warned not to open for business today, a demand to which they bowed. Unemployed men near Waterloo, Iowa, patrolled suburban roads with signs bearing the slogan, "Farmers' holiday—sell no products." . . .

The strike in this State is scheduled to last thirty days, or until its leaders have decided that farmers are paid what they should be paid for hogs, corn, wheat, chickens, cream and other products. . . .

In Kingsley, in the last few days milk and cream have been poured out of several trucks after the drivers defied demands to stop handling produce. . . .

In Harrison County, in the extreme west central part of Iowa, officials were on the alert to prevent the carrying out of threats to dump cargoes of milk trucks bound for Omaha. Notes threatening drivers were pinned to the machines.

Sioux City, Iowa, August 15.—Continued activity of milk producers and live-stock raisers on highways entering this city again resulted in disorders and injuries to drivers of trucks today. Scores of trucks loaded with milk, farm products and live stock headed towards Sioux City have been turned back on nearly every highway after the drivers have been warned in no uncertain manner.

More than forty trucks were halted at the Woodbury County line north of the city, where hundreds of farmers had gathered. A few trucks crashed through a steel cable which was stretched across a bridge, but were blocked a second time when railroad ties were thrown under the wheels.

Some of the trucks returned home with their loads, but drivers of others said they would attempt to reach Sioux City by another route.

Sheriff John A. Davenport has indicated that he may deputize a hundred special officers to handle the situation. It is reported the Sheriff of Plymouth County and his deputies also may ask for help.

On demand of livestock commission men, packing house interests at the Sioux City stock yards and produce dealers, whose receipts have been materially cut, a conference was held today attended by their representatives, the Sheriff's forces, the police and State agents.

A demand for a large force of deputies was made. It was also proposed that Governor Turner be asked to order National Guard troops out for protection.

Lemars, Iowa, April 27, [1933].—District Judge Charles

C. Bradley was dragged from his court room this afternoon by a crowd of more than 600 farmers. They slapped him, blindfolded him and carried him in a truck a mile from the city, where they put a rope around his neck and choked him until he was nearly unconscious. His face was smeared with grease and his trousers were stolen.

The abduction followed Judge Bradley's refusal to swear he would sign no more mortgage foreclosures.

The farmers had entered his court room to discuss with him hearings which are to determine the constitutionality of two new laws relating to mortgage foreclosures.

The judge requested them to take off their hats, and to stop smoking cigarettes.

"This is my court," he said.

At his words the farmers, wearing bandanna handkerchiefs over their faces, arose, hauled him off the bench, slapped him and shook him, and finally carried him bodily out of the court house onto the lawn.

There they made their demand that he would swear that he would not sign any more foreclosure actions. Judge Bradley, who is about 60 years old, defied the crowd and was jeered and again slapped.

Next they put him on a truck and drove to a crossroad, where they reiterated their demands, but the judge continued to refuse.

A rope was then put about his neck, and when some one gave it a pull Judge Bradley fell, only partly conscious, but still refusing to comply with the request.

The farmers then dragged him to his feet, carried him to the side of the road and threw the loose end of the rope over a sign, but Judge Bradley defied them to "go on."

"Make him get down on his knees and pray," one of the farmers shouted.

The judge was pushed to his knees.

"I will do the fair thing to all, to the best of my knowledge," he said.

One of the farmers removed a hub-cap from a truck and placed it on the judge's head.

Oil and grease from the cap ran down his face and the farmers threw dirt on him, which stuck to the oil.

After the "prayer" the farmers removed Judge Bradley's trousers and filled them with dirt from the roadside. Then they drove off, leaving the begrimed jurist standing in the middle of the road.

# — Document No. 25 —

# INCIDENTS INVOLVING THE SOUTHERN TENANT FARMERS' UNION*

*Abhorring organization of any kind among laborers, the Southern landlords particularly resented a common union of whites and blacks, putting class above race distinctions. Incidents of April, 1935, and November, 1936, and the sorry plight of dispossessed sharecroppers in Missouri's bootheel in 1939, conclude these documents.*

⚹          ⚹          ⚹

Memphis, Tenn., April 15 [1935].—The city of Marked Tree, a community of about 2,000 inhabitants, half of whom are Negroes, squats among the cotton fields of Northeastern Arkansas about forty miles from Memphis, on the inadequate banks of the St. Francis River. Since the first of the year it has been the scene of much of the mob violence in which, the workers say, the landlords and riding bosses of the big plantations have resorted in their effort to stamp out the seeds of unionism sown among their sharecroppers by Socialist organizers.

There on March 25 a band of forty-odd masked night-riders fired upon the home of C. T. Carpenter, attorney for the Southern Tenant Farmer's Union and an old-time Southern Democrat whose father fought with General Robert E. Lee in the Army of the Confederacy.

* From *The New York Times*, April 16, 1935; *ibid.*, November 29, 1936; *ibid.*, January 11, 12, 1939.

The raid upon Mr. Carpenter's home was the climax to a series of similar attacks upon the homes of Negro members of the union.

On March 30 an armed band of vigilantes mobbed a group of Negro men and women returning home from church, beating several of them with pistol butts and flashlights. That same night in the neighboring town of Lepanto night riders shot out all the lights in a Negro church, terrorizing the women and children of the congregation.

Just over the Poinsett County line . . . is the town of Birdsong, where on March 16 Norman Thomas and a group of his followers were threatened with violence and run out of town.

The whole section has been in the grip of a perfervid hysteria which probably would have resulted in a massacre before this if the union had not heeded its attorney's advice to stop holding meetings and to obey the laws . . . invoked by the planters and their elected public officials to curb the union, which has a membership of about 4,000 representing about a third of the sharecroppers in the region.

Little Rock, Ark. [Nov. 28, 1936.]—Conviction yesterday of Paul D. Peacher, city marshal of Earl, on a charge of slavery arose out of an investigation made by "G" men from Washington who spent some weeks in Arkansas after farm tenancy disturbances in Crittenden County last Spring. Evidence was presented that Peacher, claiming a contract to clear school district lands, accosted Negroes on the streets of Earl and arrested eight for vagrancy. These men he arraigned in the court of Mayor T. H. Mitchell, who convicted them and imposed jail sentences. Peacher, alleging a verbal contract with the county judge through the county Sheriff for using city prisoners, took the Negroes to a stockade he had erected on school property, working them until they were ordered liberated by Governor J. M. Futrell. Peacher was indicted upon this testimony.

At the trial in the . . . Federal Court at Jonesboro it developed that Peacher paid the county nothing for the prisoners' work, and the court records failed to disclose

any contract. It was also proved that the Negroes were
not vagrants but that some owned their own homes.

In spite of this the jury hesitated to convict. After an
hour and a half it reported to Judge John E. Martineau
that it was unable to reach a verdict.

Exasperated, Judge Martineau . . . directed a verdict
of guilty and told the jury it should not be influenced by
the fact that a white man was on one side and Negroes on
the other. Within a few minutes the jury returned with a
verdict of guilty, but with a plea that Peacher not be given
a jail sentence. Judge Martineau, however, sentenced him
to a fine of $3,500 and two years in prison, with the
qualification of probation instead of prison if the fine was
paid.

Southern States have for many years leased prisoners
to farmers and contractors upon the payment of their
fines to the city or county, and in Arkansas by one county
to another, where a county conducts a penal farm.
Peacher's offense was the first prosecution under a law
passed in 1866. Crittenden County has been the hotbed of
farm tenancy disturbances and there officers of the Farm
Tenant Union from Memphis claim they were flogged by
plantation owners. A suit for $100,000 against prominent
East Arkansas men filed by these alleged victims was
scheduled for trial at this term of court in Jonesboro, but
was continued due to costs for services not having been
paid by the plantiffs. . . . The Farm Union disturbances
flared often in the Jonesboro trial, the defense insisting
that Northern union agitators had made such a furor over
alleged conditions prior to the national election that
President Roosevelt was forced to direct an investigation
by the Department of Justice which was naturally expected to dissipate after the election. District Attorney
Isrig insists that the planters subscribed a large fund for
the defense of Peacher, who was active in their interests
during the tenancy controversy.

New Madrid, Mo., Jan. 10, [1939].—Hundreds of
share-cropper families, both Negroes and whites, who fled
or were rescued from their shanties during the great flood
two years ago this month, were homeless again tonight
under different but similarly pitiful circumstances.

This time they bundled up their few possessions and

trekked from their rickety homes to the highways in a mass demonstration against working conditions in the Southeast Missouri bootheel country. Saying they were forced from their homes by eviction notices and by other causes beyond their control, they united to bring their plight to the attention of the nation.

The mass migration followed an appeal by Owen H. Whitfield, Negro Baptist minister. Along 100 miles of . . . U. S. Highways, 60 and 61, more than 1,000 men, women and children camped in the open air. They huddled around campfires or makeshift stoves along desolate rights-of-way, sharing the contents of huge steaming kettles. . . .

Men feeble with age, one woman so ill she had to be carried on a cot, and babies crying from fright and hunger added to the distressing picture.

No violence or disorder was reported. The croppers were instructed by their leaders to be courteous, and each group has a camp policeman who also is spokesman. . . .

William H. Jones, a sharecropper declared they were being evicted because of the landowners' desire to switch from tenants to day labor to eliminate the necessity of sharing government crop reduction payments with renters.

New Madrid, Mo., Jan. 11.—Huddled tonight around flickering roadside campfires, hundreds of Southeast Missouri sharecropper families, demonstrating against a low economic status, defied probable rain or snow, shrinking food supplies and the danger of disease.

Many of the ragged army of more than 1,000 men, women and children, most of them Negroes, were ill-prepared to face the predicted inclement weather.

Tents and improvised shelters of bed clothing offered little protection from the chilly wind which ushered in their second night in the open air.

The march to the highways was called as a protest against the growing movement in the cotton country to abandon sharecropping in favor of the employment of day laborers. Leaders of the demonstration contended that some landowners had evicted their renters to avoid sharing crop benefit payments with them.

Various landowners in the "bootheel" area blamed the situation on Missouri's tremendous gain in farm population in recent years, restricted cotton acreage, the shift from manual labor and mule power to modern motorized farming, and losses suffered by some operators under the sharecropper system.

Many former croppers, "day hands" during the recent cotton season, were in the groups whose camps were scattered along 150 miles of United States Highways 60 and 61.

Will Travers, leader of a group at Hayti, said all of his followers had been day laborers on farms in Pemiscot County, "but we can't live on 75 cents a day."

Having nowhere to go, the workers heeded the urging of such leaders as Owen H. Whitfield, Negro farmer and part-time Baptist minister, and trekked with their meager possessions to the highways.

Sewing machines, dressers, tables and beds were stacked along the roads in disarray. Groups took turns sleeping in dilapidated automobiles. Others slept on cornshuck mattresses or blankets.

A few had oil-barrel stoves and the familiar rural pot-bellied iron stoves to provide warmth and heat for preparing meals. Some of the more provident brought cooking chickers with them, but fat pork, bread and coffee was the fare for the majority of the refugees.

# A SHORT BIBLIOGRAPHY

Baldwin, Leland D., *Whiskey Rebels* (Pittsburgh, 1939).

Bassett, John S., "The Regulators of North Carolina, 1765-1771," *American Historical Association Annual Report,* 1894 (Washington, 1895), pp. 141-212.

Benson, Lee, *Merchants, Farmers, and Railroads, 1850-1877* (Cambridge, 1955).

Bond, Beverley W., *Quit-Rent System in the American Colonies* (New Haven, 1919).

Buck, Solon Justus, *The Granger Movement . . . , 1870-1880* (Cambridge, 1913).

Capper, Arthur, *The Agricultural Bloc* (New York, 1922).

Cheyney, Edward P., *The Anti-Rent Agitation in the State of New York, 1839-1846* (Philadelphia, 1887).

Church, Thomas, *The History of the Great Indian War of 1675 and 1676, Commonly Called Philip's War* (new edn., New York, 1860).

Destler, Chester McArthur, *American Radicalism, 1865-1901* (New London, Conn., 1946).

Du Bois, James T., and Gertrude S. Mathews, *Galusha A. Grow, Father of the Homestead Law* (New York, 1917).

Fine, Nathan, *Labor and Farmer Parties in the United States, 1828-1928* (New York, 1928).

Fisher, Commodore B., *The Farmers' Union* (Lexington, Ky., 1920).

Haynes, Fred E., *Third Party Movements Since the Civil War* (Iowa City, 1916).

Hicks, John D., *The Populist Revolt* (Minneapolis, 1931).

Kester, Howard, *Revolt Among the Sharecroppers* (New York, 1936).

Kile, Orville M., *The Farm Bureau Movement* (New York, 1921).

Kramer, Dale, *The Wild Jackasses: The American Farmer in Revolt* (New York, 1956).

McConnell, Grant, *The Decline of Agrarian Democracy* (Berkeley and Los Angeles, 1953).

Mather, Increase, *The History of King Philip's War;* Cotton Mather, *A History of the Same War* (Boston, 1862).

Minot, George Richards, *The History of the Insurrections in Massachusetts in the Year Seventeen Hundred and Eighty Six and the Rebellions Consequent Thereon* 2d edn., Boston, 1810).

Mitchell, Wesley Clair, *A History of the Greenbacks* (Chicago, 1903).

Morlan, Robert L., *Political Prairie Fire: The Nonpartisan League, 1915-1922* (Minneapolis, 1955).

Saloutos, Theodore, and John D. Hicks, *Agricultural Discontent in the Middle West, 1900-1930* (Madison, Wis., 1951).

Simkins, Francis B., *The Tillman Movement in South Carolina* (Durham, 1926).

Steen, Herman, *Coöperative Marketing* (Garden City, 1923).

Taylor, Carl C., *The Farmers' Movement, 1620-1920* (New York, 1953).

Usher, Ellis B., *The Greenback Movement of 1875-1884, and Wisconsin's Part in It* (Milwaukee, 1911).

Ward, Townsend, "The Insurrection of the Year 1794, in the Western Counties of Pennsylvania," *Pennsylvania Historical Society Memoirs,* Vol. VI (Philadelphia, 1858), pp. 117-203.

Warren, Joseph Parker, "The Confederation and the Shays Rebellion," *American Historical Review,* Vol. XI (October, 1905), pp. 42-67.

Wertenbaker, Thomas J., *Torchbearer of the Revolution: The Story of Bacon's Rebellion and Its Leader* (Princeton, 1940).

Wiest, Edward, *Agricultural Organization in the United States* (Lexington, Ky., 1923).

# INDEX

189